Waterfalls of the Pacific Northwest

Gregory Alan Plumb

The Writing Works
Seattle, Washington

Library of Congress Cataloging in Publication Data

Plumb, Gregory Alan, 1956-
    Waterfalls of the Pacific Northwest.

    Includes indexes.
      1. Hiking—Northwest, Pacific—Guide-books.   2. Camp
sites, facilities, etc.—Northwest, Pacific—
Directories.   3. Waterfalls—Northwest, Pacific—
Description.   4. Northwest, Pacific—Description and
travel—Guide-books.   I. Title.
GV199.42.N69P58   1983   917.7   83-1261
ISBN 0-916076-60-1

Published by The Writing Works
417 East Pine Street
Seattle, Washington 98122
The Writing Works is a part of the Cone-Heiden Group

TABLE OF CONTENTS

PREFACE

Water, in its many forms, provides some of the earth's most beautiful landscapes. Rivers, lakes and coasts all offer images of scenic beauty, but undoubtedly waterfalls are the most impressive of hydrologic features. People have always been drawn to falls as places of wonder, relaxation, and inspiration.

As a youth, my first experience of this sparkling water formation was the popular *Tahquamenon Falls* on Michigan's Upper Peninsula. The shimmering waters of this block-type waterfall naturally tint to a burnt orange during its descent. Our family so enjoyed this waterfall that we began including stops at other falls in our itinerary on vacations "up north." However, we had difficulty finding waterfalls other than those marked by "point of interest" symbols on the state highway map. Even these were not always easy to find.

As an adult, my interest in waterfalls was strengthened when I moved to northern Idaho. The Pacific Northwest was a new region to be explored, and on many trips I discovered waterfalls. After visiting a few, I wanted to see more. Unfortunately I discovered that no text had been written on the subject. At that point an idea was kindled. This recreational guidebook is the result.

This book is dedicated
to my parents,
Arnold and Marguerite Ann Plumb.

ACKNOWLEDGMENTS

Many sources contributed directly or indirectly to this guidebook. I would like to recognize them here.

In compiling an inventory of waterfalls prior to field investigations, I scanned the 7½-minute and 15-minute series of topographic maps printed by the U.S. Geological Survey. U.S. Forest Service maps provided a secondary reference. I reviewed these map collections in the University of Idaho library. The cooperation of social science librarians Dennis Baird and Gail Eckwright is greatly appreciated. Additional falls were discovered from book sources, including Harvey Manning's *Footsore: Walks and Hikes Around Puget Sound* series; S.R. Bluestein's *Hiking Trails of Southern Idaho*; and E.M. Sterling's *Trips and Trails* series. A few waterfalls were encountered during field travels. Rangers or local residents mentioned others, and I stumbled on some by accident.

The most enjoyable part of preparing this book was, of course, seeking out the falls of the Pacific Northwest. The personnel at ranger stations of the National Park Service and U.S. Forest Service were very helpful in providing road and travel information. I also want to thank the following individuals for their assistance: Sheldon Bluestein of Boise; Mark Dellinger of Klamath Falls, Oregon; Terry Eckwright, Paul Kimmell, Brian Raber, and Meg Van Dyck of Moscow, Idaho; Wayne Jenkins of Ashton, Idaho; Bill Rember of Stanley, Idaho; and Bob Stengel of Durand, Michigan. Thanks also to the many outdoorspeople met along trails and befriended at campfires. Their positive comments about the need for a waterfall guidebook sustained my ambition to finish the project. Also, my 1965 Ford Falcon, which traversed over 15,000 miles, deserves a citation for performance beyond the call of duty!

Geologic, cultural, and historical information was primarily obtained through library research, although some facts were gathered in the field. Geologic sources included *Cascadia: The Geologic Evolution of the Pacific Northwest*, by Bates McKee; *Geology of Oregon*, by E.M. Baldwin; *Humid Landforms*, by Ian Douglas; *Guide to the Geology and Lore of the Wild Reach of the Rogue River*, by William Purclom; *Catastrophic Flooding: The Origin of the Channeled Scabland*, edited by Victor R. Baker; and *Geologic Map of Mount Rainier National Park*, by R.S. Fiske, C.A. Hopson, and A.C. Waters. An exhaustive array of cultural and historical trivia was found in *Oregon Geographic Names*, by L.A. McArthur; *The Idaho Encyclopedia*, a Federal Writers' Project; and *Origin of Washington Place Names*, by Edmond Meany.

Most of the photographs in the guidebook were taken by the author. Charley Knowles, Jr., of Moscow, Idaho, and Chris Harrington of Lawrence, Kansas, prepared the prints for publication. I hope this culmination of a lifelong fascination will be useful to the many people who share my love of waterfalls.

INTRODUCTION

Welcome to the waterfalls of the Pacific Northwest! This book has been written as a field guide to lead you to falls of all shapes and sizes. Whether you want an afternoon trip or an extensive vacation, a short walk or a backpacking trek, this guidebook will tell you where to find the waterfalls. Extraordinary adventures await you!

But first, a warning. The grandeur of waterfalls is accompanied by an element of risk. Accidents can occur at even the most developed locations, particularly when youngsters are left unsupervised or people forget their sanity and unduly place themselves in dangerous situations. The keys to safe and sane travel to and about waterfalls are:

1) Do not stray from fenced observation points or trails in steep areas.
2) Remain aware of your surroundings when taking pictures, and don't startle others when they are concentrating on photography.
3) Stay away from sloping, unvegetated surfaces.
4) Remember each party member's limitations concerning steep climbs, long trails, or undeveloped areas. Turn back whenever you feel insecure about the route ahead.
5) If you must travel alone, be sure someone knows your travel plans.

Hundreds of waterfalls are described in this guidebook. They are grouped into 14 geographic regions for easy use. Introductory comments for each region describe the physical setting for waterfall development. The regions are divided into subsections with falls descriptions, most with maps showing the descents' locations.

Many of the falls described here have no official names, so for convenience I have called them by the names of their streams or of nearby landmarks. Physical, cultural, historical, and geological information is included when known. Symbols accompanying each description show the relative accessibility, a subjective rating, and the general shape or form of the falls. Public campgrounds are shown on many of the maps within the book. Also, it is permissible to pitch camp at almost any location on National Forest land as long as you carry an ax, shovel, and bucket for fire control.

Some falls in this book are located on private property. The traveler must exercise added responsibility in these areas. A landowner may decide **not** to grant access subsequent to the publication of this book. No Trespassing signs should be heeded.

Camping, hiking, and backpacking are not described in this book, since a great variety of paperbacks are available on these subjects. But when hiking, you should at least carry the "Ten Essentials"—sunglasses, knife, matches, fire-starter, first aid kit, flashlight, compass, a map, extra clothing, and extra food. Use a day pack or rucksack. And remember, **please don't litter.** Pick up after careless individuals who have come before you. The cleaner you leave our environment, the more beautiful and enjoyable it will be.

ACCESSIBILITY SYMBOLS

 Located within one-fourth mile of a road accessible by passenger vehicle. If not visible from the road, a well-developed trail leads to the falls.

Located within one-fourth mile of a road recommended for four-wheel drive vehicles. If not visible from the road, a well-developed trail leads to the falls.

Located more than one-fourth mile from a road accessible by passenger vehicle. Developed trails provide good access for day hikers.

Located many miles from a road accessible by passenger vehicle. Developed trails provide access for backpackers with supplies for overnight or multiple night camping.

Located in an undeveloped area. These are accessible from unmaintained pathways or by walking up drainages. See text for details on individual falls. A strong pair of hiking boots is recommended. **Not** recommended for young children and may be risky for nervous adults or those with physical limitations.

 Located adjacent to a lake, reservoir, or secluded river.

Accessible by some type of watercraft.

Some falls may have more than one of the symbols in order to further define accessibility. In these cases a diagonal line connecting the symbols represents the word "or." A horizontal connecting line represents "and." Examples:

Accessible for ambitious day hikers, but backpacking is recom – mended for leisurely jaunts.

Accessible by hiking more than one- half mile from a road recommended for four-wheel drive vehicles.

STARRED RATING SYSTEM

This is a subjective rating determined by the form and height of a waterfall, and by the scenery surrounding it. When viewing several descents in a short time, it is best to see the less spectacular ones first, then progress to the better falls.

 Exceptional, awe inspiring.

Very Good, many of these would seem exceptional if not compared to the higher-rated falls.

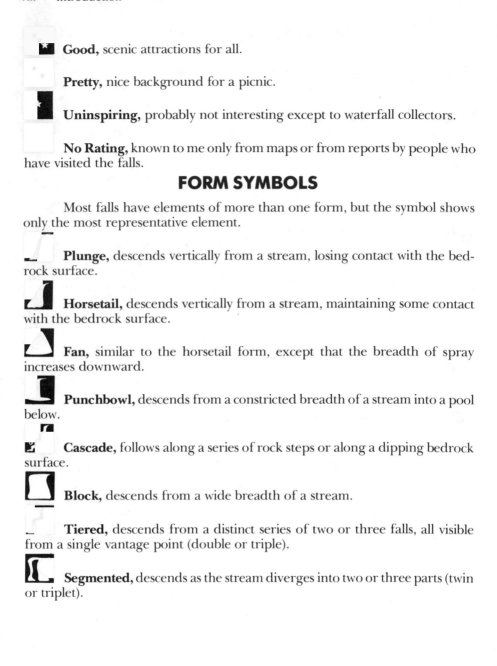

Good, scenic attractions for all.

Pretty, nice background for a picnic.

Uninspiring, probably not interesting except to waterfall collectors.

No Rating, known to me only from maps or from reports by people who have visited the falls.

FORM SYMBOLS

Most falls have elements of more than one form, but the symbol shows only the most representative element.

Plunge, descends vertically from a stream, losing contact with the bedrock surface.

Horsetail, descends vertically from a stream, maintaining some contact with the bedrock surface.

Fan, similar to the horsetail form, except that the breadth of spray increases downward.

Punchbowl, descends from a constricted breadth of a stream into a pool below.

Cascade, follows along a series of rock steps or along a dipping bedrock surface.

Block, descends from a wide breadth of a stream.

Tiered, descends from a distinct series of two or three falls, all visible from a single vantage point (double or triple).

Segmented, descends as the stream diverges into two or three parts (twin or triplet).

THE MAPS

When used correctly, the maps in this book will lead you to the waterfalls with a minimum of confusion. First, use a highway map to find the general vicinity of the waterfall. For falls away from a main highway, pinpoint its location with one of the book's detailed subsection maps. For easy comparison, each map has north oriented upward. Check the accuracy of your odometer, and make allowances if it is off. For a rough gauge of hiking distances, remember that an average persons takes half an hour to hike one mile. The map key below shows the symbols used throughout the book.

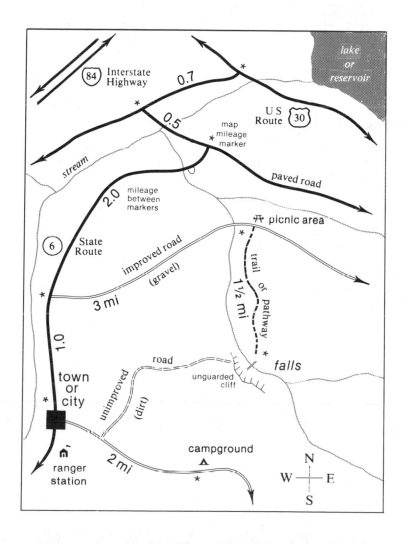

Snoqualmie Falls

THE NORTH CASCADES
OF WASHINGTON

The Cascade Range extends from British Columbia through Washington and Oregon to northern California. A progression of spectacular volcanic peaks tower above the range from north to south, starting with Mount Baker, Mount Rainier, and Mount Adams in Washington; Mount Hood, Three Sisters, and Mount McLaughlin in Oregon; and Mount Shasta in California. Since the Cascades encompass a large part of the Pacific Northwest and contain many waterfalls, the range has been divided into six chapters in this book.

The North Cascades include the central portion of Washington starting at Interstate 90, which crosses Snoqualmie Pass, and covering the mountains north to the Canadian border. This region features three large national forests, three wilderness areas, two national recreation areas, and North Cascades National Park. Of the 90 falls mapped within the region, 52 are described in the following pages.

Aside from two volcanoes, Mount Baker and Glacier Peak, most of the mountains of the North Cascades are older than those of the range's southern extension. The North Cascades form a rugged and complex arrangement of various nonvolcanic materials. Large masses of granite are distributed within the region. Other rock forms found in the area include gneiss and schists. These rock types vary from 50 million to 500 million years in age, but their arrangement in the general mountainous terrain as seen today is due to uplifting over the past ten million years.

Intensive glaciation accounts for the great relief from the region's peaks to its valleys. Four major periods of glacial activity occurred from 10,000 years to two million years ago. The heads of glaciers eroded into the mountains, sharpening their peaks, and extended to lower elevations, deepening and widening valleys.

The abundance of waterfalls in the North Cascades is largely due to the glacial scouring of the Range's bedrock surfaces. Many descents plummet into *glacial troughs,* or valleys. *Wallace Falls* and *Rainbow Falls* (near Lake Chelan) are stunning examples. Others skip and bounce off rock walls into the troughs, for instance, *Bridal Veil Falls, Gate Creek Falls,* and *Preston Falls.*

Sometimes cataracts are associated with a rounded depression previously carved by the upper portion of a glacier. Water may pour into this *cirque* from ridgetops, or tumble from its outlet into a trough. *Falls of Horseshoe Basin* and *Twin Falls* (at Twin Falls Lake) are classic descents of this type.

Glaciers may erode unevenly when carving out their *U*-shaped troughs. The streams which presently occupy the valley floors are called *misfit streams* and have falls where sharp drops occur. These descents are generally less dramatic than the types previously mentioned. Representative falls of this form include *Sunset Falls* and *Teepee Falls.*

1

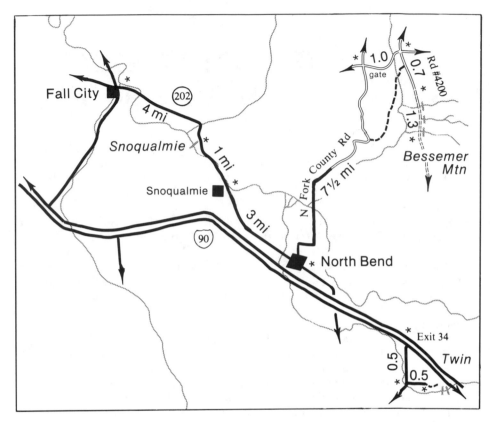

NORTH BEND AREA

This area has examples of falls in different settings and with various levels of accessibility. At one extreme, *Snoqualmie Falls* is a well-developed tourist site complete with a picnic area, viewing platform, lodge, and restaurant. On the other hand, although *Twin Falls* has its own state park, the site is not easily reached, and the park has no facilities. The *Falls from Bessemer Mountain* are even more remote.

Snoqualmie Falls

This 268-foot plunge is one of Washington's most visited scenic attractions. Puget Sound Power and Light Company is to be commended for preserving the integrity of the falls while diverting enough of the Snoqualmie River to produce hydroelectric power for 16,000 homes. The waterfall is next to S.R. 202 between Fall City and Snoqualmie.

Twin Falls

Presently only a view of the 75 to 100-foot lower portion of this double descent is sanely possible. The descent is also known as *Upper Snoqualmie Falls.* Leave Interstate 90 at Edgewick Road (Exit 34) and follow 468

Avenue SE for half a mile. Turn left (east) at SE 159 Street to its end. You are now at the entrance to the undeveloped and unpublicized Twin Falls State Park. When I surveyed this entry, the three-fourths-mile trail ended just before the falls came into view. If this is still the case, climb the ridge to your left, descend its other side, and ford the South Fork Snoqualmie River to its east bank facing the base of the lower descent.

Falls from Bessemer Mountain

Three separate falls crash down from unnamed creeks toward North Fork Snoqualmie River. At North Bend turn onto North Fork County Road and drive 7½ miles to East Spur Gate 10. If the gate is closed, backtrack 2½ miles to a hiking trail which leads across the North Fork. If the gate is open, drive one mile to the next major junction and turn right (south) on Road #4200. Keep driving for three quarters of a mile, then continue on foot up the steep route which passes the falls. The last of the three waterfalls is 1¼ miles farther.

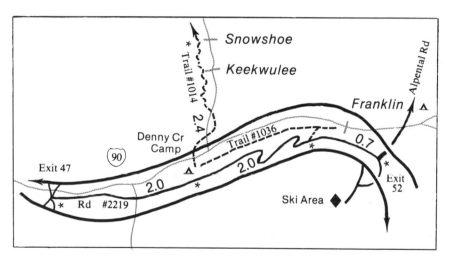

SNOQUALMIE PASS

This area's main campground has the unfavorable distinction of being between lanes of Interstate 90! Actually it's not as bad as it sounds, but the soft murmur of speeding traffic detracts from the natural setting. The campground, named Denny Creek, is the point of departure to the surrounding falls. Leave I-90 at Snoqualmie Pass Recreation Area (Exits 47 and 52) and follow Denny Creek Road #2219 for two to three miles to the camp.

Keekwulee Falls

Begin hiking at Denny Creek Trailhead #1014 on the north side of the camp. Cross South Fork Snoqualmie River once and Denny Creek twice, the second time in 1½ miles. The trail ascends steeply half a mile farther to the falls. Keekwulee is a Chinook word meaning "falling down."

Snowshoe Falls

Continue hiking along Trail # 1014 for almost half a mile past Keekwulee Falls to this descent from Denny Creek. Snowshoe Falls and Keekwulee Falls were named in 1916 by The Mountaineers, a regional association for outdoor recreationists.

Franklin Falls

Start hiking at Franklin Falls Trailhead # 1036 at the east end of the camp. After a leisurely 1½-mile jaunt, reach a 70-foot falls on South Fork Snoqualmie River. An alternative route to the falls is via the historic Snoqualmie Pass Wagon Road. This route intersects Road # 2219 about two miles east of the camp and leads to the falls in less than 300 yards.

LEAVENWORTH AREA

Downtown Leavenworth is a place of Old World character. The traditional storefronts and the surrounding alpine setting are reminiscent of Bavaria. Enjoy seasonal activities such as the Mai Fest, Autumn Leaf Festival, and Christmas Lighting.

Drury Falls

Fall Creek drops over the cliffs of Tumwater Canyon into the Wenatchee River. For views of the cataract from across the river, drive six miles northwest of Leavenworth along U.S. 2. The site is one mile southwest of Swiftwater Picnic Area.

LAKE WENATCHEE

Lake Wenatchee is a popular vacation area for family camping. There are several campsites on the eastern shore. Drive 14 miles northwest of Leavenworth along U.S. 2 to S.R. 207, then five miles north to the lake. All the area's falls are located a short ways upriver from the lake.

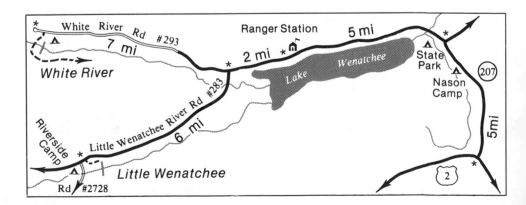

Franklin Falls

Little Wenatchee Falls

Turn off S.R. 207 onto Little Wenatchee River Road #283. In six miles Road #283 meets with Rainy Creek Road #2728. Park at the junction and find an undesignated trail about 150 feet away. A short walk farther, Little Wenatchee River tumbles over a series of rock steps.

White River Falls

Although this 60 to 100-foot cataract is near a roadway, you must hike to find a good view. Drive to the end of White River Road #293. Follow Panther Creek Trail #1502 across White River, then downstream. In one mile, a spur trail to the left leads to good views of the falls. At White River Falls Campground, adults can climb on chunks of bedrock for obstructed overviews of the descent. Be careful! This is definitely not a place for fooling around.

STEVENS PASS

Many waterfalls beckon from the roadside as you drive west on U.S. 2 over the 4,061-foot elevation of Stevens Pass.

Deception Falls

Deception Creek steeply cascades 30 to 60 feet. Drive to Deception Falls Picnic Area eight miles west of Stevens Pass and ten miles east of Sky-komish. There is a parking area across the highway from the falls.

Alpine Falls

A very short trail leads to the top of this 30 to 50-foot descent. Drive about 1½ miles west from Deception Falls Picnic Area. Park at the turnout just past the bridge crossing Tye River. Determined bushwhackers can find good views of Alpine Falls by hiking down the slope to the river from the far end of the turnout.

INDEX

Eagle Falls

Drive about nine miles west of Skykomish, or four miles east of Index to the parking turnout closest to mile marker 39. A path immediately east of the marker leads to a noisy 25 to 40-foot cascade along South Fork Skykomish River. National Forest maps incorrectly show this descent at the site of Canyon Falls, which is actually farther downstream.

Canyon Falls

The geology of this descent is very interesting. Granite, which is common in the North Cascades region, decomposes grain by grain when united

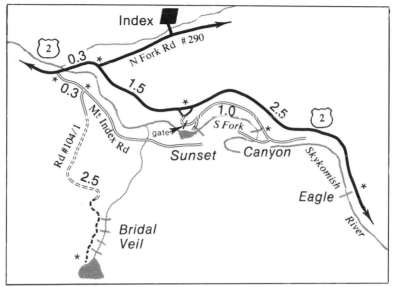

Canyon Falls

with water. As a stream flows over granitic outcrops, its boulders are chemically smoothed and hollowed by the water, often in unusual shapes. South Fork Skykomish River has physically eroded and widened a fracture in the granite to form Canyon Falls, dramatically illustrating how running water can modify a landscape both chemically and physically.

Turn off U.S. 2 between mile markers 36 and 37 about 1½ miles east of Index and 2½ miles west of Eagle Falls. Follow the private road about an eighth of a mile and park where a gate blocks the way. The falls is about one mile down the drive. Bear left at the fork at the start of the walk. Closeup views are possible, but be careful. Stay away from the slippery, moss-covered boulders and bare rocks that slope toward the river.

Sunset Falls

The South Fork slides 60 to 100 feet in impressive fashion. Follow the instructions to Canyon Falls, but take the right fork at the beginning. The descent is a few minutes away. For views from the other side of the river, drive along Mount Index Road, which is described in the next entry.

Bridal Veil Falls

Water pours off Mount Index in four parts, each descending 100 to 200 feet along Bridal Veil Creek. Leave U.S. 2 at Mount Index Road immediately south of the bridge over South Fork Skykomish River. Turn right (south) in 0.3 mile on Road #104/1. Only high clearance vehicles can follow the entire 1.5-mile length of the road. Most automobiles park after one mile. A hiking trail begins at the road's end and ascends moderately to the first of the cataracts in one mile. The falls are also visible as silvery white threads from the main highway.

GOLD BAR

Wallace Falls State Park, opened in 1977, is destined to become a popular attraction along the U.S. 2 corridor. Leave the highway at Gold Bar and follow the signs two miles to the park.

Wallace Falls

Wallace River drops 250 feet, making the falls one of the tallest in the North Cascades. The trail leading to it is called Woody Trail after Frank Woody, a former state senator and lifelong outdoorsman.

The trailhead to the cataract begins past the campsite area. It soon diverges, the right fork ascending moderately, while the left goes up at a gentler rate. The trails converge after one mile on the steeper path or two miles on the gradual path. There is a picnic area and a first view of the falls a short distance farther, and a favorite viewpoint half a mile beyond. The trail continues up above the falls to a vista of the Skykomish Valley.

ROESIGER LAKE

Explorer Falls

Drive 13 miles north from Monroe on Woods Creek Road to cottage-lined Roesiger Lake. Or reach the lake by driving about eight miles south from Granite Falls on Lake Roesiger Road. Turn on the gravel Monroe Camp Road from Lake Roesiger Road. Avoid spur roads as you leave and reenter wooded tracts. After 3½ miles, park at a gravel pit on the right side of the road. Hike upstream a few hundred feet to an exposed view of an unnamed tributary of Woods Creek dropping 50 to 70 feet from a cliff. The descent is perfect for taking an invigorating shower.

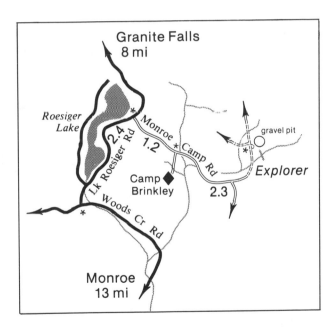

GRANITE FALLS

This community is named after cascades located 1½ miles north of town on S.R. 92, also called the Mountain Loop Highway.

Granite Falls

Water froths along South Fork Stillaguamish River in a series of descents totaling 30 to 40 feet. A short trail leads to the falls from a parking area on the south side of a bridge crossing the river. A 580-foot fishway connects the top and bottom parts of the river via a 240-foot tunnel, allowing salmon to bypass the cascades and procede upstream to spawn.

VERLOT

Waterfalls abound in this area where creeks flow from Mount Pilchuck into the South Fork of the Stillaguamish. Follow S.R. 92 ten miles northeast from Granite Falls to Verlot Ranger Station and town site. After the main road crosses the South Fork about three-fourths mile east of the ranger station, make two successive right turns—the first on Pilchuck State Park Road #3014, the second on gravel Monte Cristo Grade Road #3003.

First Falls

This descent has no official name, but it is the initial falls encountered along Road #3003. The cataract drops along an untitled creek crossed half a mile beyond the turnoff from Pilchuck Road.

Heather Creek Falls

Less than half a mile west of First Falls is a series of descents along Heather Creek.

Triple Creek Falls

Road #3003 ends next to this drop. A 40-foot upper descent is accessible by climbing a few hundred feet up a trail near the creek.

Twentytwo Creek Falls

This is a series of three descents accessible from hiking trails within Lake Twentytwo Research Natural Area. Continue along S.R. 92 past Pilchuck Road #3014 for three-fourths mile to the designated Twentytwo Creek Trailhead #702. The lowest falls is encountered after half a mile of moderately steep hiking. Follow a short spur trail to view the two other descents.

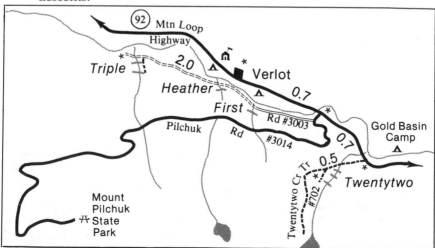

TWIN FALLS LAKE

Twin Falls

Spend the day hiking to a unique double falls whose waters pause between descents in minuscule Twin Falls Lake. Wilson Creek drops 125 feet into the pool, then tumbles another 400 feet from the outlet. The trail system on this state-owned land was built by the Department of Natural Resources.

Drive about five miles east of Verlot Ranger Station along S.R. 92 to Road #3015, labeled Bear Lake Trail and Bald Mountain Trail. In 2¾ miles turn right (east) at the junction of Road #3015B. Drive to the next fork in 1½ miles and turn left at the Bald Mountain Trail Sign. Ignore the many short spurs along the final 1¼ miles. Turn right at the Y in a quarter mile, then left again in another three-fourths mile. The Bald Mountain Trailhead is located at the end of this steep quarter-mile road.

Hike three-fourths mile along Bald Mountain Trail to Beaver Plant Lake. Soon after, take the right fork on Ashland Lakes Trail. Pass both Upper and Lower Ashland Lakes in two miles. There are campsites at both lakes. Twin Falls Lake and its falls are 1½ miles beyond Lower Ashland Lake.

Wallace Falls

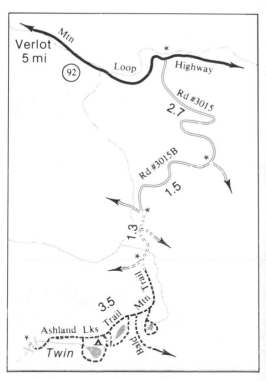

ARLINGTON AREA

Ryan Falls

This waterfall is located on private property, but can be seen from the main highway. Water slides 50 to 75 feet down a hillside along an unnamed creek. Take S.R. 530 almost seven miles northeast from Arlington. The descent, just west of mile marker 28, is at its best during late autumn, according to the landowner.

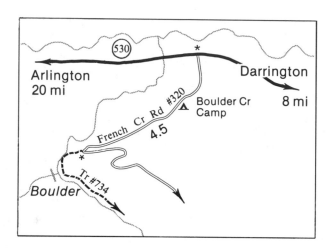

BOULDER CREEK

Boulder Falls

An unnamed creek curtains 80 feet over a cliff into Boulder Creek. Turn off S.R. 530 onto French Creek Road #320, located eight miles west of Darrington, or 20 miles east of Arlington. After 4½ miles, the gravel road takes a sharp turn. The Boulder Creek Trail #734 sign is at the apex of the bend. The falls is an easy one-mile walk ahead across the river from the trail. This descent is incorrectly marked on National Forest and USGS topographic maps.

SAUK RIVER DRAINAGE

Asbestos Creek Falls

Follow Clear Creek Road #3210 from Darrington south to Clear Creek Camp in three miles. Turn right at the camp. Asbestos Creek flows beneath the gravel road in 2½ miles. The steep cascades are a few hundred feet upstream.

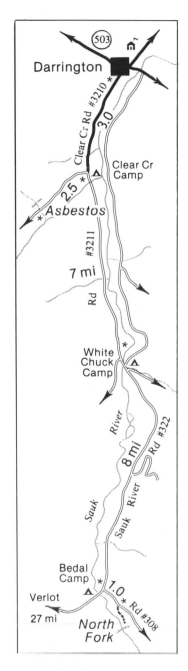

Cedar Creek Falls

North Fork Falls

Start out as to Asbestos Creek Falls, but instead of turning at Clear Creek Camp, continue straight on Road #3211. Turn onto Sauk River Road #322 and follow it to North Fork Road #308 a total of 15 miles beyond Clear Creek Camp. Turn on Road #308 and drive one mile to the sign for Trail #660. Hike a quarter mile to the falls on North Fork Sauk River. North Fork Road can also be reached from Verlot. Drive east 27 miles along Mountain Loop Highway, which begins as S.R. 92.

SUIATTLE RIVER DRAINAGE

Suiattle Falls

This double cascade falls a total of 70 to 100 feet along an unnamed creek from Suiattle Mountain. Take the Darrington-Rockport Road to the bridge crossing the Sauk River. About a quarter mile east of the bridge, turn on Suiattle River Road #345. Drive 2¾ miles along Road #345 to a turnout on the right side of the road. Walk to the drainage just crossed and scramble 100 feet upstream to the falls. The descent has no official name, so I have called it by the name of the nearby mountain and river.

Teepee Falls

From previously listed Suiattle Falls, continue along Suiattle Road #345 for four miles. Teepee Falls is a 50 to 60-foot series of cascades located directly under the bridge spanning the chasm of Big Creek.

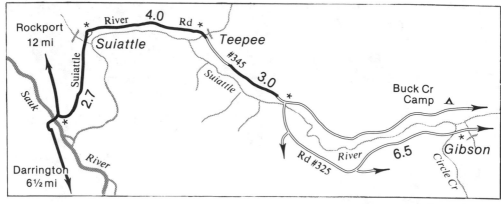

Gibson Falls

This narrow fan of water glistens in a dimly lit recess. From Teepee Falls, continue three miles to Suiattle River next to the junction of Road #325. The falls is hidden along an unnamed creek 6½ miles up Road #325. A dip in the bridge over Circle Creek is a good reference point. Drive 0.1 mile past this point to the next drainage. Follow the creek upstream 200 feet to the base of the falls.

SAUK VALLEY

Marietta Falls

This 100 to 125-foot double waterfall plunges at the end of its final descent. Leave S.R. 20 at Sauk Valley Road one mile west of Concrete. The road soon crosses the Skagit River and reaches Marietta Creek in eight miles. Park at the undesignated area immediately west of the bridge. The falls is a quarter mile upstream. The hike is enjoyable, but requires fording the creek once or twice and climbing over a small rock outcrop to the base of the falls.

MOUNT BAKER

Mount Baker is the dominant feature of the North Cascades. This glacier-covered volcano rises thousands of feet above the surrounding mountains. Meltwater from its northeast-facing glaciers is the source of water for the following descent.

Rainbow Falls

At Concrete, turn north from S.R. 20 onto Baker Lake Highway #11. In 15 miles, turn left (west) on Morovitz Creek Road #1130. Pass Baker Hot Springs in 3.3 miles, and take the right fork from Road #1130 half a mile beyond. A half mile down this gravel road Rainbow Creek pours 150 feet into a gorge. The upper half of the falls is visible from an overlook 40 feet from the road, but the rest is hidden by vegetation and the canyon escarpment.

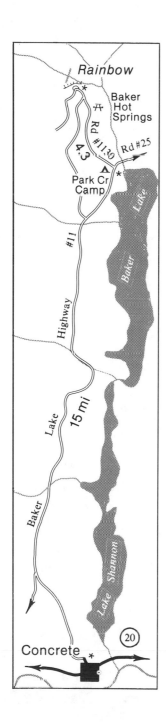

NOOKSACK RIVER

Nooksack Falls

To reach this explosive waterfall, drive 34 miles east of Bellingham along S.R. 542 to the hamlet of Glacier and continue seven miles east to Wells Creek Road #403. Turn here and drive half a mile to partial overviews of the falls. Do not cross the bridge over Nooksack River or you will miss the descent. Perhaps the owner, Puget Sound Power and Light, will someday construct an observation platform to offer more dramatic views of this raging torrent.

ROSS LAKE NATIONAL RECREATION AREA

North Cascades National Park is bisected by Ross Lake National Recreation Area and its three reservoirs—Gorge Lake, Diablo Lake, and Ross Lake. Reach this rugged portion of Washington via the North Cascades Highway (S.R. 20), normally open June through October.

Ladder Creek Falls

This series of falls is unique because Seattle City Light illuminates it at night with colored lights. Park at the east side of Newhalem and follow the bridge and trail across Skagit River and behind the Gorge Powerhouse. The descents are in a landscaped rock garden.

John Pierce Waterfall

Water slides 400 to 500 feet into Diablo Lake. Board a Seattle City Light tugboat at Diablo Dam or launch your own craft at Colonial Creek Campground. This cataract is also known as *Pierce Falls* and *Horsetail Falls*.

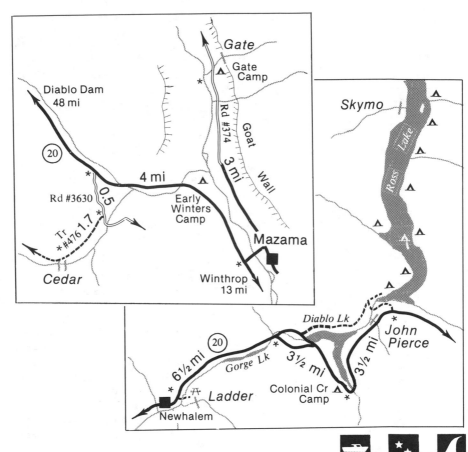

Skymo Creek Falls

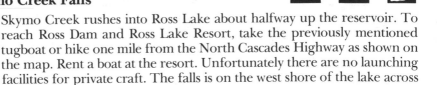

Skymo Creek rushes into Ross Lake about halfway up the reservoir. To reach Ross Dam and Ross Lake Resort, take the previously mentioned tugboat or hike one mile from the North Cascades Highway as shown on the map. Rent a boat at the resort. Unfortunately there are no launching facilities for private craft. The falls is on the west shore of the lake across from aptly named Tenmile Island.

METHOW VALLEY

Mazama is the eastern outpost for travel along the North Cascades Highway. It has the last facilities for 75 miles for westbound travelers. There are two attractive falls in the Mazama area.

Cedar Creek Falls

The creek has cut deeply into granite bedrock to form this series of 20 to 30-foot descents. Drive four miles past Mazama along S.R. 20 and turn left (south) on Sandy Butte-Cedar Creek Road #3630. Follow this gravel route for half a mile and park near the marked Cedar Creek Trail #476 leading to the right. The trail ascends moderately 1.7 miles to the falls.

Gate Creek Falls

This 100-foot descent skips down a portion of Goat Wall, a glaciated cliff rising 2,000 feet above the Methow Valley floor. Drive to Gate Creek Camp, located three miles northwest of Mazama along West Fork Methow Road #374. Find the creek at the far side of the campground. Walk a quarter mile upstream to a steep *talus* (rocky) *slope*. Scramble up this jumble to get a view of the stream's descent from Goat Wall.

CHEWACK RIVER DRAINAGE

Falls Creek Falls

Drive north on Chewack Road #392 to Falls Creek Campground 11½ miles from the frontier-style town of Winthrop. An access trail along the south side of the creek leads shortly to the 30-foot major descent of the lower falls. Faulted (fractured) bedrock above the base of Chewack Valley causes the stream to descend in a series of cascades.

Chewack Falls

Chewack River explodes 30 feet over granite benches to form this waterfall. Drive one mile past the appropriately named Thirtymile Campground to the end of Chewack Road #392. Hike 2.8 miles up Chewack Trail #510 to the falls.

FOGGY DEW CREEK

Foggy Dew Falls

Turn off of S.R. 153 onto Gold Creek Road #3109 about halfway between the towns of Twisp and Pateros. Turn left (south) after five miles on Foggy

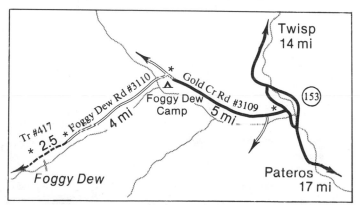

Rainbow Falls

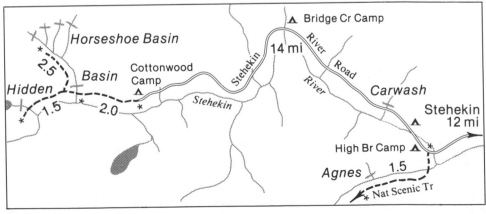

Dew Creek Road #3110. The trailhead is four miles farther at the end of the road. A moderate 2½-mile hike along Foggy Dew Trail #417 brings you to the falls where water accelerates 100 feet through a narrow chute.

LAKE CHELAN

Lake Chelan is a classic example of a large *paternoster lake*. It is the result of a *terminal moraine* formed by the accumulation of rock debris deposited at the end of a glacier. The glacier carved out the Chelan Valley 10,000 to 12,000 years ago. The moraine acts as a natural dam for meltwater entering the valley from the adjacent snow-laden mountains. The lake is 51 miles long and attains a depth of over 1,500 feet. It is one of the largest alpine lakes in the continental United States.

Rainbow Falls

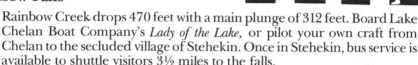

Rainbow Creek drops 470 feet with a main plunge of 312 feet. Board Lake Chelan Boat Company's *Lady of the Lake,* or pilot your own craft from Chelan to the secluded village of Stehekin. Once in Stehekin, bus service is available to shuttle visitors 3½ miles to the falls.

Bridal Veil Falls

This 50 to 75-foot descent is distantly visible from the tour boat on the return trip from Stehekin to Lucerne. Bridal Veil Falls earns a higher rating if you have a private boat which can approach it more closely.

Domke Falls

Water rushes 30 to 50 feet into Lake Chelan from Domke Creek. The tour boat passes near the falls on the return trip from Lucerne to Chelan. The descent and the creek are named for the first settler in the vicinity.

NORTH CASCADES NATIONAL PARK

While the majority of national parks within the continental United States have developed routes for motorized travel, North Cascades National Park remains overwhelmingly wilderness in character. The remote Stehekin River Road, one of only two gravel roads entering the park, allows access to five falls in the park's southeast sector. Take the ferry boat from Chelan to Stehekin. A shuttle service transports hikers and backpackers to various campsites and trailheads along the road.

Amazingly, there are no symbols for falls on the USGS topographic maps of the national park. Perhaps the remoteness of the North Cascades explains this omission. I would not be surprised if the area actually has hundreds of waterfalls.

Agnes Falls

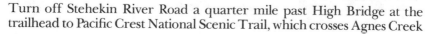

Turn off Stehekin River Road a quarter mile past High Bridge at the trailhead to Pacific Crest National Scenic Trail, which crosses Agnes Creek and enters into Glacier Peak Wilderness in one mile. Half a mile farther an unnamed creek can be seen falling 100 to 140 feet into the opposite side of Agnes Creek Gorge.

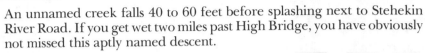

Carwash Falls

An unnamed creek falls 40 to 60 feet before splashing next to Stehekin River Road. If you get wet two miles past High Bridge, you have obviously not missed this aptly named descent.

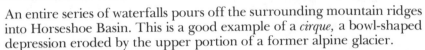

Basin Creek Falls

Take a shuttle bus to its farthest destination at Cottonwood Camp. Hike two miles west from the camp to a 125 to 175-foot descent of Basin Creek.

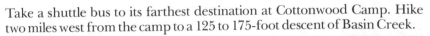

Falls of Horseshoe Basin

An entire series of waterfalls pours off the surrounding mountain ridges into Horseshoe Basin. This is a good example of a *cirque*, a bowl-shaped depression eroded by the upper portion of a former alpine glacier.

From Basin Creek Falls, continue hiking for half a mile to a fork in the trail. Bear right and follow switchbacks steeply upward, meeting Basin Creek in less than half a mile. The basin and falls are 1½ miles farther.

Hidden Falls

Hike on the main trail to the fork to Horseshoe Basin, but take the left fork and continue one mile to a crossing of Doubtful Creek. The 75 to 120-foot waterfall is a short distance upstream.

ENTIAT VALLEY

Apple orchards are common along the fertile plain of the lower Entiat Valley. Farther upstream the valley becomes less gentle and the orchards give way to coniferous forest. The upper valley has three scenic, though not overwhelming waterfalls.

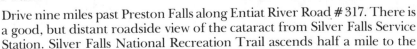

Preston Falls

Preston Creek slides 75 to 100 feet down the mountainside. To reach it, turn off U.S. 97 onto Entiat River Road #317 less than one mile south of Entiat. Reach Ardenvoir in 8½ miles and the falls 13½ miles farther, approximately 1¼ miles past Entiat Valley Ski Area.

Silver Falls

Drive nine miles past Preston Falls along Entiat River Road #317. There is a good, but distant roadside view of the cataract from Silver Falls Service Station. Silver Falls National Recreation Trail ascends half a mile to the base of the cliff from which Silver Creek drops 100 to 140 feet. The trail is dedicated to J. Kenneth and Opal F. Blair, stewards of public lands during the 1950s and 1960s.

Entiat Falls

The Entiat River breaks over a rock ledge and thunders 30 feet to boulders below. The waterfall is most impressive during spring high water periods. Drive three miles northwest of Silver Falls to Entiat Falls Viewpoint. Entiat is an Indian word meaning "rapid water."

Silver Falls

THE OLYMPICS AND VICINITY

The Olympic Peninsula is dominated by the mountains which rise 6,000 to 8,000 feet above its coastal margins. This abrupt relief causes moist air masses moving into the area to produce some of the highest annual precipitation in the continental United States. Normal figures reach 140 inches of rain on the Pacific Coast and 40 feet of snow in the high mountains. Most precipitation occurs from November to April.

Many small glaciers lie on the northern flanks of the highest mountains. Meltwater from the glaciers as well as from snowfields feeds the region's rivers and streams during the drier summer season. As a result, basins throughout the Olympics drain liberally year-round. An abundance of water flowing over a mountainous landscape dissected by glaciation has created many waterfalls throughout the peninsula.

The Olympic Mountains are quite youthful geologically. The range was formed by forced uplift of a contact zone between two large *crustal plates* of the earth's exterior. The collision of these plates began about 70 million years ago and has continued the mountain-building process to the present. During the four Ice Age episodes between two million and 10,000 years ago, alpine glaciers stretched to lower elevations than today, carving large *U*-shaped valleys. Major rivers presently rush along the base of these glacial troughs, sometimes descending over rocks which erode at unequal rates. More common are the falls created when tributary streams pour over the steep sides of glacial troughs on their way to the valley floors.

Gigantic continental glaciers played an important role in shaping Puget Sound and the Strait of Juan de Fuca. The Laurentide Ice Sheet covered almost all of Canada and the northern tier of the eastern United States about 10,000 years ago. A lobe of this massive glacial system extended into western Washington and gouged out large expanses of the former "Puget Lowland." As the glacier retreated, ocean water inundated the land areas which had been eroded below sea level. The familiar water bodies known today are the result.

Vashon, Bainbridge, Whidbey, and Camano islands to the east and the San Juan Islands to the north represent erosional remnants of the preglacial landscape. They were not denudated, or eroded away, by the Puget Lobe.

ORCAS ISLAND

The San Juan Islands are one of the most beautiful archipelagos in the world. Orcas Island, the largest of the chain's 172 islands, has four miniature waterfalls. Board a Washington State Ferry at Anacortes. After an enjoyable 1½ hours spent churning across Puget Sound, get off at Orcas Landing. Follow Horseshoe Highway 12¾ miles north, passing the hamlets of Westsound, Crow Valley, and Eastsound before arriving at Moran State Park. Drive 1¼ miles within the park to a turnout at a marked trailhead. The waterfalls drop along Cascade Creek.

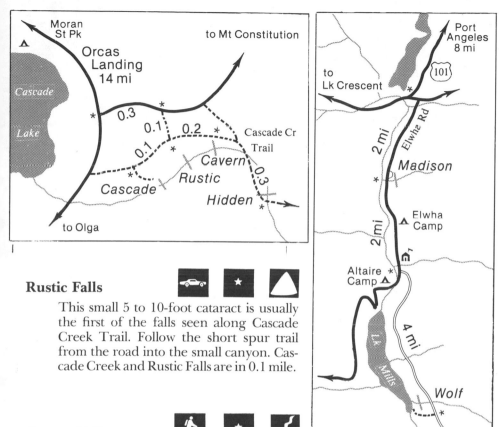

Rustic Falls

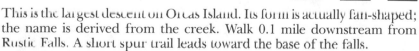

This small 5 to 10-foot cataract is usually the first of the falls seen along Cascade Creek Trail. Follow the short spur trail from the road into the small canyon. Cascade Creek and Rustic Falls are in 0.1 mile.

Cavern Falls

Water steeply tumbles here into a recess in the canyon. Walk upstream from the previous entry for less than a quarter of a mile. The 20 to 40-foot descent is to the right of the trail.

Hidden Falls

This 15 to 20-foot drop is "hidden" only if you are not observant. Continue walking upstream along Cascade Creek Trail. Cross the creek twice. The second crossing is above the top of the descent.

Cascade Falls

This is the largest descent on Orcas Island. Its form is actually fan-shaped; the name is derived from the creek. Walk 0.1 mile downstream from Rustic Falls. A short spur trail leads toward the base of the falls.

ELWHA

Olympic National Park is best known for its lush rain forest valleys and snow-topped mountains, but some beautiful waterfalls also deserve attention.

Madison Creek Falls

Most motorists will never see this obscure 40 to 50-foot cataract. Turn off U.S. 101 at the marked Elwha Valley entrance. Drive two miles to the park boundary and stop at an undesignated turnout to the left (east). A short walk from the road into a wooded tract brings the falls into view.

Wolf Creek Falls

This is a double falls, but only the 30 to 40-foot lower descent is clearly visible. The 50 to 70-foot upper portion is hidden by the gorge. Drive two miles beyond the park boundary, turning left past the ranger station onto a gravel road. In four miles, park along the turnout at the marked trailhead to Lake Mills. Follow the trail steeply to its end in 0.4 mile. Walk around the ridge to the right to Wolf Creek. The base of the falls is easily reached by going upstream less than 100 feet.

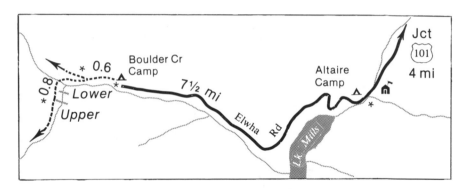

MOUNT CARRIE AREA

To reach the trail system leading to the following falls, stay on the paved Elwha Road to its end. The north shore of Lake Mills is two miles past the ranger station. Boulder Creek Camp and Trailhead is 7½ miles farther.

Lower Boulder Creek Falls

Follow the trail past the campsites to a fork in 0.6 mile. Turn left, hiking along South Fork Boulder Creek. The trail ascends moderately for 0.6 mile, then intersects a short spur trail leading to the falls. Water cascades 25 to 35 feet in Boulder Creek Gorge.

Upper Boulder Creek Falls

Continue along Boulder Creek Trail for a quarter mile past the lower descent to a second marked spur trail. The short path leads between a set of falls. Upstream are 15 to 25-foot cascades, while downstream the top of a 75 to 100-foot plunge is visible.

LAKE CRESCENT

Marymere Falls

Falls Creek plunges and horsetails 90 feet over a rock wall. Drive 14 miles west from Elwha Valley on U.S. 101 or eight miles east from Fairholm. Storm King Visitor Center and Ranger Station, across the highway from Lake Crescent, is the starting point for Marymere Falls Nature Trail which leads three-fourths mile to the falls. Take a self-guided tour or accompany a scheduled group.

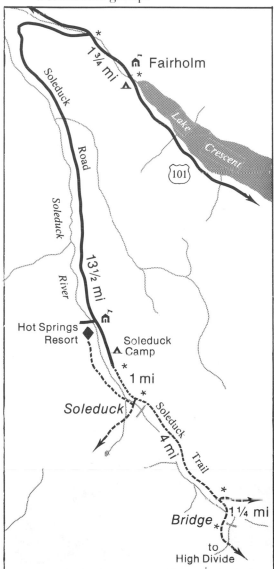

Lower Boulder Creek Falls

SOLEDUCK

There are two descents along the Soleduck River drainage. Drive 1¾ miles west of Fairholm on U.S. 101 to Soleduck Road, which leads to Soleduck Hot Springs resort in 12 miles and the road's end 1½ miles farther.

Soleduck Falls

Soleduck Falls

The Soleduck River turns at a right angle, where its waters rush 40 to 60 feet downward. Hike one mile from the Soleduck Trailhead at the end of the paved road, then turn right (south). The falls can be seen from the footbridge crossing the river. Soleduck is an English variant of the Indian phrase "Sol Duc," meaning "magic waters."

Bridge Creek Falls

Obtain a backcountry permit at Soleduck Ranger Station and proceed along Soleduck Trail, passing the junction to Soleduck Falls in one mile. Travel four miles farther to a second fork. Bear right, heading toward Soleduck Park and High Divide. The trail crosses the river in one mile and follows Bridge Creek. The cataract is less than a quarter mile away. Campfires are prohibited in this area of the park. A portable stove is a necessity if you plan to cook.

BEAVER CREEK

Beaver Falls

Beaver Creek tumbles 30 to 40 feet in three sections across an 80-foot wide rock escarpment. Turn off U.S. 101 at Sappho 12 miles north of Forks and 17 miles west of Fairholm. Follow the northbound secondary road two miles to an undesignated turnout 0.1 mile past Beaver Creek bridge. A short, unimproved path leads to the base of the cataract.

HOKO RIVER

Hoko Falls

The calm water of the Hoko River momentarily rushes 5 to 10 feet at a narrow spot where an erosion-resistant rock constricts the stream. Follow S.R. 112 to the seaside village of Clallam Bay. Continue 5½ miles west, then turn left (south) toward Ozette Lake. Drive 6¼ miles to the Hoko River and park near the bridge. Fishing access paths descend to the base of the falls.

ENCHANTED VALLEY

This entry is for all the waterfall enthusiasts who also like to backpack. Enjoy! The Enchanted Valley in the southern part of Olympic National Park is accessible only to backpackers. The most popular access route to the trail is 23 miles east of Quinault. For an alternate point of departure from Dosewallips Camp, see DOSEWALLIPS.

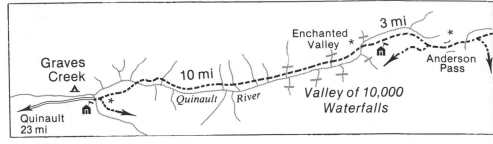

Valley of 10,000 Waterfalls

Many visitors and long-time residents of the Olympic Peninsula prefer the name "Valley of 10,000 Waterfalls" to the more common "Enchanted Valley." Although the number of descents may be exaggerated in the name, you will be hard-pressed to keep track of the scores of waterfalls seen during a single day's journey in this valley. Practically every tributary encountered along Enchanted Valley Trail breaks into a waterfall as it enters the Quinault River's glacially carved valley. Varied vegetation completes the serene scenery of the gorge.

Secure a backcountry permit at Graves Creek or Dosewallips ranger station. A ranger station in the Enchanted Valley is open during the summer if you need information or assistance.

QUILCENE AREA

Falls View Falls

Turn off U.S. 101 at Falls View Camp four miles south of Quilcene and nine miles north of Brinnon. A short trail at the south end of the campground leads to a fenced vista high above the canyon floor. An unnamed creek drops 80 to 120 feet into Big Quilcene River. The flow is best during the wet season from autumn to spring. It may disappear entirely during droughts. The descent is also known as *Campground Falls*.

DOSEWALLIPS

The eastern portion of Olympic National Park is an ideal spot for those who wish to avoid crowds. The lack of paved access roads discourages many travelers. Turn off U.S. 101 at the sign for the Dosewallips Recreation Area one mile north of Brinnon.

Dosewallips Falls

Water pours 100 to 125 feet over and around boulders along Dosewallips River. Drive 14.2 miles west from U.S. 101 to the signed turnout at the base of the cataract three-fourths mile beyond the park boundary.

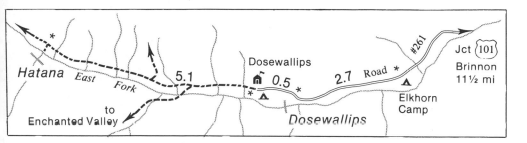

Hatana Falls

Start at the ranger station at the Dosewallips River Trailhead. Don't forget to obtain a backpacker's permit. After 5.1 miles, a marked primitive spur trail leads to a view of Hidden Creek falling from the other side of the canyon into Dosewallips River.

BRINNON

Rocky Brook Falls

Drive three miles from U.S. 101 on Road #261, or stop on the return trip from the Dosewallips area. Park at the undesignated turnout on the west side of Rocky Brook bridge. A well-worn trail quickly leads to the base of the falls. Water thunders 100 to 125 feet over a massive scarp. I've called this waterfall by the name of its stream.

KAMILCHE

Kennedy Falls

Turn off U.S. 101 onto Old Olympia Highway 2½ miles south of Kamilche/S.R. 108 and 4¼ miles northwest of the junction of U.S. 101 and S.R. 8. Drive three-fourths mile to the dirt road south of Kennedy Creek. Stay on the primary route for 2¾ miles, turning right (toward the creek) at all major forks. Park at a jeep trail and hike down the trail for half a mile to the emerald-tinted gorge of Kennedy Creek.

The best views of the falls are from the north side of the valley. Walk a short distance upstream to an easy ford above the upper descent. Then progress downstream to open, unfenced vistas. The upper portion of this small, but pleasantly tiered waterfall drops 5 to 10 feet into a pool. A little lower the creek pours 20 to 30 feet into a tight gorge.

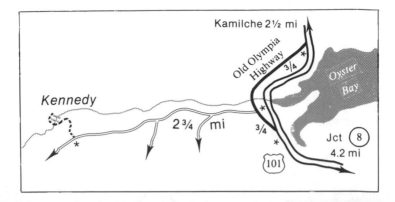

Kennedy Falls

OLYMPIA

Leave Interstate 5 at Exit 103. Olympia Brewery and visitor parking are one block east of the freeway. Paths lead through the landscaped setting of Tumwater Falls Park past four cataracts. Afterwards, take an interesting tour through the brewery and enjoy a complimentary glass of beer or soda in the hospitality room.

Upper Tumwater Falls

The form of this 10 to 20-foot drop is defined by previous alterations made to harness water power. The descent is near the picnic area along the Deschutes River.

Olympia Falls

Purified water is returned to Deschutes River from the brewery as a nice display totaling 40 to 60 feet. From the upper falls, walk downstream a short distance past the bridge over the river. The trail eventually crosses the river and passes between the upper and lower portions of this descent.

Middle Tumwater Falls

Water tumbles 15 to 25 feet along Deschutes River a short distance downstream from Olympia Falls.

Tumwater Falls

This 40-foot waterfall has been made famous by its likeness on the label of the brewery's products. Walk to a vista overlooking the falls. A footbridge crosses above the descent.

The waterfall was originally named *Puget Sound Falls* in 1829 and retitled *Shute's River Falls* in 1841. Michael Troutman Simmons led a party of American settlers to the vicinity in 1845. He coined the word Tumwater based on a Chinook word. The Indians called running water "tumtum" because they felt its sound was like the throb of the heart.

RAINBOW FALLS STATE PARK

Rainbow Falls

A large pool at the base of this 5 to 10-foot waterfall serves as a popular swimming hole. The descent of the Chehalis River is at the entrance to Rainbow Falls State Park next to S.R. 6. Interpretive trails guide the visitor through the park's stands of virgin timber.

Myrtle Falls

MOUNT RAINIER REGION

The Mount Rainier Region of Washington is among the most scenic in North America. The mountain, called Takhoma by the Yakima Indians, is the area's centerpiece, but it has many other beautiful natural features. Mount Rainier National Park, my favorite, has 122 recognized waterfalls within and near its boundaries. Of these, 66 are described in the following pages.

This is a land of fire and ice. The oldest rocks predate Mount Rainier itself. Between 30 and 60 million years ago, the region was part of a large, low-lying coastal zone scattered with terrestrial and subterranean volcanoes. These ancient volcanoes deposited thick accumulations of lava which played an important part in the formation and composition of the Cascade Range. Ten to 30 million years later, continued volcanic activity brought molten material toward the earth's surface, but most of the *magma* cooled before it could pour from the vents as lava. The bedrock formed from the *magma* became surface material when it was thrust upward by internal earth forces or was exposed by the erosion of its overburden.

Therefore, the landscape on the periphery of modern Mount Rainier is distributed with different rocks which streams erode at unequal rates. *Silver Falls* occurs where Ohanapecosh River intersects resistant vertical layers of basalt before continuing along relatively weak *volcanic breccia,* formed when lava intermingled with sandstone and siltstone. Another example is *Lower Stevens Falls,* where magma was injected into an older rock complex. The resulting bedrock proved to be more resistant than neighboring material.

Mount Rainier formed one to five million years ago and is composed of interlayering of andesitic lava and volcanic ash from repeated eruptions. One large lava flow blocks the northward course of Maple Creek, diverting the stream eastward. Coincidentally, a vertical break in the local topography, called a *fault,* was positioned along the stream's redefined route. *Maple Falls* currently descends from the fault.

The abundance of waterfalls in the region is due not to the processes described above, but to the large scale landscape modifications achieved by glaciers. A total of 27 named glaciers surround Mount Rainier today; 10,000 years ago these awesome spectacles, the earth's greatest erosive agents, extended to much lower elevations.

A topographic feature common to areas of high relief is a *step,* formed where an alpine glacier gouges its valley floor unevenly. *Clear Creek Falls* and *Sylvia Falls* are along breaks probably formed in this manner. Waterfalls from *hanging vallyes* are also common around Mount Rainier. These are formed because small, tributary glaciers cannot erode their valleys as deeply as can the large, main glaciers. Therefore a smaller glacial valley will be high above a main glacial valley floor where they meet. *Comet Falls* and *Spray Falls* are dramatic examples of this type.

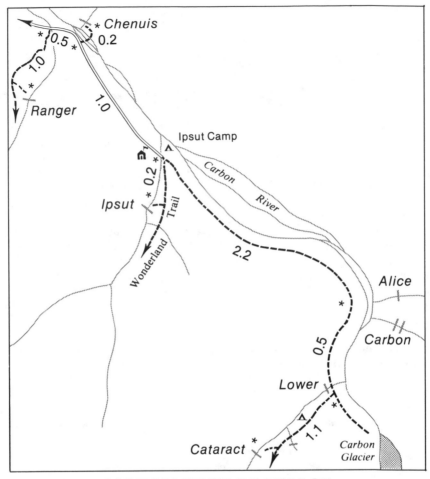

CARBON RIVER DRAINAGE

Vacationers visiting the region for the first time usually overlook this portion of Mount Rainier National Park, favoring instead better known locations like Sunrise and Paradise. Since the northwestern part of the park is frequented mostly by locals, it has been called "Our Own Little Corner of the Mountain." But wherever you are from, you will be warmly welcomed.

Drive to the city of Buckley on S.R. 410 or S.R. 162, then turn south along S.R. 162/165 through the historic mining towns of Wilkeson and Carbonado. Follow paved S.R. 162 to the park entrance along the Carbon River 12 miles past Carbonado. The road turns to gravel at the entrance.

Ranger Falls

These falls tumble a total of 100 to 125 feet along Ranger Creek. Their form is eye-catching because the lower portion splits into twin descents. Drive three miles past the park entrance to Green Lake Trailhead. The trail ascends moderately for about one mile to a marked spur which leads shortly to the falls.

Chenuis Falls

  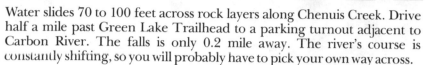

Water slides 70 to 100 feet across rock layers along Chenuis Creek. Drive half a mile past Green Lake Trailhead to a parking turnout adjacent to Carbon River. The falls is only 0.2 mile away. The river's course is constantly shifting, so you will probably have to pick your own way across.

Ipsut Falls

This double falls along Ipsut Creek totals 40 to 60 feet. Drive just past the campground to the trailhead at the end of the road. Turn right (south) on Wonderland Trail a little way from the trailhead, and follow it for a short distance to a designated spur trail leading to the falls. Please stay on the trail since the creek serves as the water supply for the camp.

Carbon Falls

Hike 2.2 miles from Ipsut Camp on the unnamed trail that follows Carbon River. Soon after you leave the forested area and catch sight of the slopes across the river, the waterfall comes into view—first the lower descent, then the upper portion. This waterfall is best viewed during the afternoon. It's rating decreases during the low water periods of late summer. Also, *Alice Falls* is located along an adjacent drainage, but is well hidden by the surrounding vegetation.

Lower Cataract Falls

These 50 to 75-foot falls along Cataract Creek are best viewed from the footbridge 2.7 miles past Ipsut Camp on the unnamed trail that follows Carbon River toward Carbon Glacier.

Cataract Falls

From the lower falls, follow the right (west) fork at the trail junction. The left fork goes to the toe of Carbon Glacier, which extends to a lower elevation than any other glacier in the continental United States. Hike 1.1 miles to a designated spur trail leading to the 50 to 75-foot falls. Also, hidden close to the main trail is a miniature waterfall. Take a shower in it if you dare!

MOWICH LAKE AREA

Drive to the city of Buckley via S.R. 410 or 162 and turn south on S.R. 162/165 to Wilkeson and Carbonado. Three miles past Carbonado, turn right on the gravel extension of S.R. 165. This road has imposing views of Mount Rainier. It ends at Mowich Lake in 16 miles.

Spray Falls

Spray Falls

This enormous display descends 300 to 350 feet and is 50 to 80 feet wide. Reach it by a leisurely hike of less than 2½ miles. Follow the Wonderland Trail 0.4 mile from Mowich Lake, then turn left on Spray Park Trail and follow it for 1.6 miles. Finally, turn right at Spray Falls Trail. An exciting view of the falls is 0.3 mile farther.

ST. ANDREWS CREEK

Enter the national park at the Nisqually entrance and continue about one mile on S.R. 706 to West Side Road. This gravel road may eventually be discontinued for vehicular use. If so, the waterfall will be accessible only to backpackers.

Denman Falls

Drive 11 miles to St. Andrews Creek, parking on the near side of the bridge. To the left is a trail which leads downstream to an observation point above the 122-foot falls. Further downstream are *Larrupin Falls* and *Ethania Falls*. Unfortunately they are not accessible.

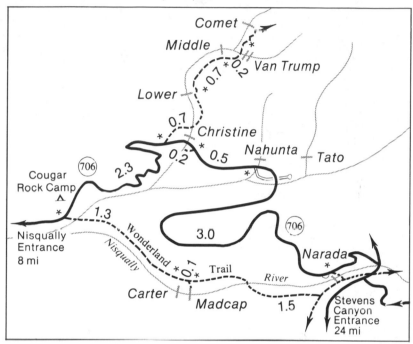

NISQUALLY DRAINAGE

The south-central part of the National Park has a wealth of waterfalls. The area is bounded on the west by Cougar Rock Campground and on the east by the entrance to the Paradise area.

Carter Falls

Get on the Wonderland Trail across the highway from Cougar Rock Camp. A sign directs you toward the falls, but first cross Nisqually River. This may require a short ford depending upon the mood of the sediment-laden water. Hike 1.3 miles up the moderate trail to the falls. This 50 to 80-foot descent is named for Harry Carter, who built much of the early Paradise Trail.

Madcap Falls

A short distance past Carter Falls an unlabeled spur trail leads shortly to these 20 to 30-foot cascades along the Paradise River. USGS topographic maps label this feature about a quarter mile farther upstream, but darned if I could see anything there resembling falls.

Comet Falls

Narada Falls

These popular falls descend 168 feet or 241 feet, depending whether the plunge at the end of the horsetail is included. Park by the road about one mile west of the entrance to the Paradise area, or continue hiking 1½ miles along the Wonderland Trail from Carter Falls. A branch of the Theosophical Society of Tacoma named the falls after their guru, Narada, in 1893.

Middle Van Trump Falls

Van Trump Creek has many series of descents. Four major falls are described in the following entries. Drive 2.3 miles east of Cougar Rock Camp to the Comet Falls Trailhead. The trail is steep but safe, ascending 1,400 feet in 1.6 miles. The roar of *Lower Van Trump Falls* can be heard after less than three-fourths mile, but the shape of the canyon hides the descent from view. The middle falls is three-fourths mile farther. Its 40 to 50-foot drop can be easily seen from a few feet off the trail.

Van Trump Falls

Don't give up hiking yet! The middle descent, double falls totaling 60 to 90 feet, is only 0.2 mile farther. And you're less than 100 yards away from the best of them all.

Comet Falls

You've made it! Before you is a spectacular 320-foot plunge. This is a classic example of a waterfall descending from a hanging valley. If you are a glutton for punishment, the trail continues for almost another mile toward the top of the falls.

Christine Falls

Drive less than a quarter mile past Comet Falls Trailhead to the turnout on the east side of the Van Trump Creek bridge. Stairs lead down from the bridge to a picturesque view of these 40 to 60-foot falls.

Nahunta Falls

These falls steeply cascade 150 to 175 feet along an unnamed tributary to Nisqually River. Park at the gravel spur half a mile east of Van Trump Creek bridge and look up the side of the slope. During low discharge periods of late summer, this descent deserves a lesser rating.

Tato Falls

Follow the previously mentioned gravel spur 0.3 mile to its end. The 40 to 60-foot waterfall is best seen from the parking area. Surrounding vegetation obscures closer views. The descent is on an unnamed tributary of Nisqually River.

Christine Falls

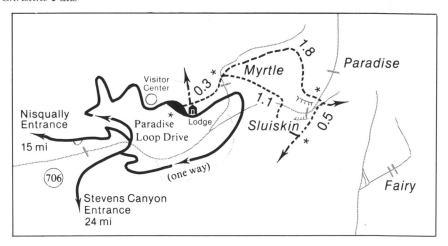

PARADISE

At 5,800 feet of elevation, Paradise is the highest point to which you can drive on the mountain's southern face. Travel 15 miles east from the Nisqually entrance or 24 miles west from the Stevens Canyon entrance along S.R. 706. The contemporary-looking Visitor's Center and the traditionally rustic Paradise Inn are halfway along the Paradise Loop Road.

Myrtle Falls

The Skyline Trail begins at Paradise Inn. Walk an easy one-third mile to Edith Creek. A stairway descends to a superb vista overlooking the 60 to 80-foot falls with Mount Rainier in the background.

Paradise Falls

Continue along Skyline Trail, passing its junction with Lakes Trail in 1.1 miles. Far away to the right in Stevens Basin, *Fairy Falls* can be faintly heard and even seen with an afternoon sun. See STEVENS CANYON for a description. Half a mile farther Skyline Trail passes Ice Cave Trailhead, Stevens-Van Trump historic monument, and then a footbridge crossing Paradise Creek. Look upstream from the bridge to the distant 30 to 50-foot drop of *Paradise Falls.*

Sluiskin Falls

This 300-foot slide along Paradise River is named for an Indian guide who aided Hazard Stevens and P.B. Van Trump in the first recorded climb of Mount Rainier in 1870. From the footbridge at Paradise River, hike a few hundred yards to a view of the top portion of the falls. Short side spurs from the trail provide full views. Children and nervous adults should stay on the main trail, since the spurs end abruptly at cliffs.

STEVENS CANYON

It is no exaggeration to say that S.R. 706 is one of the most scenic roads ever engineered. The Stevens Canyon stretch is not as convoluted as other sections of the route, but its construction was just as daring an undertaking. The view across the canyon from Wonderland Trail confirms that judgment. The fine line of the highway can be seen cut into the side of Stevens Ridge over 400 feet above the canyon floor.

Fairy Falls and Upper Stevens Falls

The large descents from Stevens Basin are not highly regarded because there are no close views of them. Drive to the turnout at The Bench, located about 5½ miles from Paradise or six miles from Box Canyon. Look up the valley toward Stevens Basin which is below and to the right (east) of Mount Rainier. Two silvery white threads drop from the Basin. Upper Stevens Falls descends 200 to 400 feet, while Fairy Falls plummets 700 feet in two major drops. Fairy Falls can also be viewed from the Skyline Trail. See PARADISE for details.

Martha Falls

Water spills 125 to 150 feet along Unicorn Creek. The highway intersects Wonderland Trail 0.8 mile north of The Bench. The trail winds moderately down 0.6 mile to a footbridge overlooking the falls.

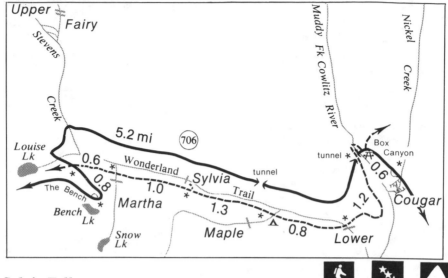

Sylvia Falls

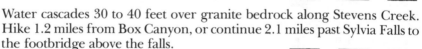

Continue past Martha Falls along the Wonderland Trail for another easily hiked mile. An undesignated, but well-worn spur trail leads shortly to the 80 to 100-foot falls spilling down a rock step on Stevens Creek.

Lower Stevens Falls

Water cascades 30 to 40 feet over granite bedrock along Stevens Creek. Hike 1.2 miles from Box Canyon, or continue 2.1 miles past Sylvia Falls to the footbridge above the falls.

Maple Falls

Hike to Maple Creek Camp, located 0.8 mile past Lower Stevens Falls and 1.3 miles east of Sylvia Falls. Start at the footbridge below the camp and head upstream for about half a mile. I did not survey this waterfall because the thick bushes prevented me from approaching it and I lacked waterproof legwear to wade through the stream.

Cougar Falls

This impressive 100 to 125-foot plunge is accessible to adults only. Drive 0.6 mile from Box Canyon to the undesignated turnout immediately north of the Nickel Creek bridge. Walk down the primitive trail to good direct views of the falls in 0.1 to 0.2 mile. Warning: Stay away from the bare rock surfaces near the creek. They slope sharply into a steep canyon!

SILVER FALLS AREA

This popular area near the southeast entrance of the park boasts hot springs and giant forest stands in addition to waterfalls. Walk a short distance from Ohanapecosh Campground to the natural setting of the hot springs. Feel dwarfed by the Grove of the Patriarchs between the Stevens Canyon entrance and Olallie Creek.

Silver Falls

Rushing water thunders 30 to 40 feet into a pool. Drive 0.3 mile south of the Stevens Canyon entrance along S.R. 123. Find the trailhead to the right (west) which shortly leads down to the bottom of the gorge and the falls along the Ohanapecosh River. Two trails from Ohanapecosh Campground also provide a leisurely one-mile stroll to the falls. There are at least three smaller descents immediately upstream and one downstream from the main falls, but limit your views to those available from the trail. The tumultuous river has claimed the lives of many who failed to heed the posted warnings in the vicinity.

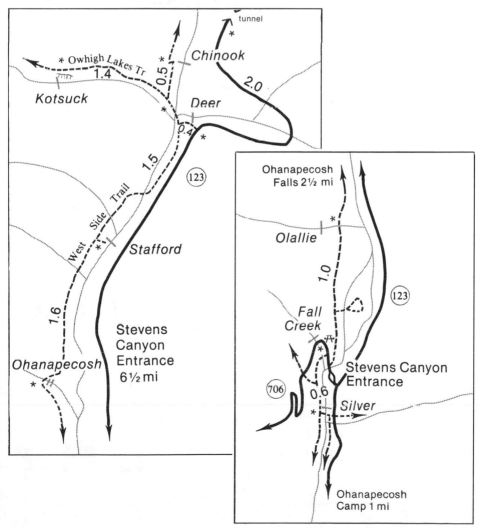

Olallie Creek Falls

Hike from the parking area near Stevens Canyon entrance or from Silver Falls. One mile north of the highway, the East Side Trail crosses Olallie Creek. The 30 to 50-foot cascades are upstream from the footbridge. I've called this unnamed waterfall after the creek.

Fall Creek Falls

Fall Creek nearly sprays onto S.R. 706 before flowing under the highway. Walk a quarter mile from the Stevens Canyon entrance parking area to see these 30 to 50-foot falls. The descent deserves a lower rating during the low water periods of late summer.

CHINOOK CREEK DRAINAGE

This pleasant collection of waterfalls lies along a sparsely used, but easily accessible trail system within the National Park. Drive to the Owyhigh Lakes Trailhead next to S.R. 123, located 6½ miles north of the Stevens Canyon entrance and 4½ miles south of Cayuse Pass. Alternatively, hikers can continue north past Olallie Creek along the West Side Trail.

Deer Creek Falls

Wind down Owyhigh Lakes Trail to Deer Creek in less than a quarter mile. Look upstream into the steeply cascading 60 to 80-foot falls. I've called this unnamed waterfall by the stream name.

Chinook Creek Falls

Trees in the foreground partially block the view of these sharp 75 to 100-foot cascades. Hike along the West Side Trail for about half a mile past the trail's north junction with Owyhigh Lakes Trail. The falls are seen just before the trail switches back uphill. I've called this unnamed descent by the name of its stream.

Kotsuck Creek Falls

Hike along Owyhigh Lakes Trail to views over the top of these falls. The trail ascends moderately for 1.4 miles past its junction with the West Side Trail. The 125 to 150-foot descent actually deserves a four-star rating, but the view from the trail is inadequate. To get a better one, retrace your steps down the trail. Then carefully make your way through the woods to the canyon rim facing the falls. Perhaps the Park Service will someday construct a spur trail providing a viewpoint for all.

Stafford Falls

Water plummets 30 to 40 feet into a large pool below. Follow the West Side Trail south from its junction at Owyhigh Lakes Trail. An easy 1½ miles later, an undesignated, but well-worn spur trail leads to this descent along Chinook Creek.

Ohanapecosh Falls

This double punchbowl waterfall drops 50 to 75 feet along the greyish waters of Ohanapecosh River. Continue past Stafford Falls for 1.6 miles to where the West Side Trail crosses the river. The best view is south of the footbridge, a few feet from the trail.

BACKPACKERS' FALLS

The extensive trail system within the National Park provides access to many of Mount Rainier's remote areas. Because the backcountry falls described here are widely scattered, it was not practical to include maps showing their locations. Instead, obtain the USGS map for Mount Rainier National Park, or use the appropriate large scale USGS maps listed with the falls. Also, remember to secure a backpacking permit at a ranger station.

Marie Falls and Mary Belle Falls

There are at least five descents within the basin of Nickel Creek, of which two have been officially named. Hike north from Box Canyon along the Wonderland Trail for 5½ to six miles. Birds-eye views of the falls are to the west (left), well past the heavily timbered region along the Cowlitz Divide ridge.

Wauhaukaupauken Falls

Continue hiking the Wonderland Trail for 1¼ to 1¾ miles past the previously described location (a total of 7¼ miles from Box Canyon). The falls are 100 feet below the shelter along Ohanapecosh River. The name, obviously of Indian origin, is reputed to be larger than the descent!

Falls of Ohanapecosh Park

At least six falls drop into the Boulder Creek drainage at Ohanapecosh Park. Climb steadily up switchbacks on the Wonderland Trail from Wauhaukaupauken Falls. A series of falls streaming from the adjacent cliffs come into view to the northeast about a mile past timberline.

Huckleberry Creek Falls

Hike three to four miles north of Sunrise to the base of these falls as shown on the topographic map.

Garda Falls

Hike six to seven miles west of Sunrise along the Wonderland Trail. The falls is immediately upstream from where the trail crosses Granite Creek.

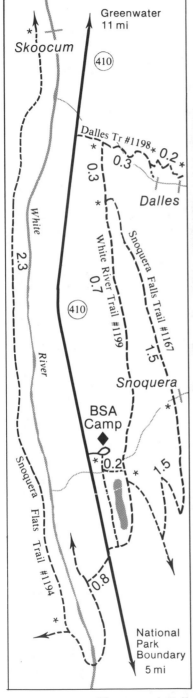

Greenwater
11 mi

410

Skoocum

White River 2.3

Dalles Tr #1198 * 0.2 *
0.3

0.3

Dalles

White River Trail #1199 0.7

Snoquera Falls Trail #1167 1.5

410

Snoquera

BSA
Camp
◆

* 0.2 *

1.5

Snoquera Flats Trail #1194

0.8

*

National
Park
Boundary
5 mi

Ohanapecosh Falls

Affi Falls

Hike five miles northwest of Sunrise, first on Wonderland Trail, then on the Northern Loop Trail The trail passes near the top of the falls where Lodi Creek descends down a glacial valley to West Fork White River.

Van Horn Falls

Hike four to five miles past Affi Falls along the Northern Loop Trail to the footbridge crossing West Fork White River. Look along the west side of the valley to see this series of three descents from Van Horn Creek.

CAMP SHEPPARD

Camp Sheppard is a Boy Scouts of America site, but visitors are welcome to use the trail system. In fact, the Scouts blazed the pathways for that purpose. The entrance to the camp is along S.R. 410, about 11 miles south of Greenwater and five miles north of the National Park.

Snoquera Falls

The impressiveness of this 200 to 300-foot waterfall decreases from spring to autumn. Follow Moss Lake Nature Trail from the parking area to the east side of the small lake. Take the designated Snoquera Falls Loop Trail #1167 to the falls in 1½ miles. Alternatively, hike from the north end of Trail #1167 via White River Trail #1199.

Dalles Falls

Each portion of this double descent can be viewed separately. Continue hiking along White River Trail #1199 to its north end, where Dalles Creek Trail #1198 is met. This trail ascends steeply, but safely through switch-backs to the top of The Dalles gorge. In one-fourth mile a short spur trail leads to the lower falls. A half mile farther the upper falls can be seen from the main trail. Both falls reduce to trickles during the low water periods of late summer.

Skoocum Falls

Take the Moss Lake Nature Trail from the parking lot to the west side of the lake. Cross the highway, then the footbridge over White River to Snoquera Flats Trail #1194. Hike 2¼ miles to where this descent of White River can be seen from the trail.

RAINIER VALLEY

For an excellent example of a *glacial trough* shaped by the enormous erosive powers of an alpine glacier, look down from Chinook Pass and admire the characteristic steep-sided, *U*-shaped form of Rainier Valley. The glacier has long since disappeared, and the Rainier Fork now flows along the valley bottom. The Pass was also formed by glacial activity. It is geomorphically known as a *col*, a notch eroded in a ridge by glaciers on either side.

Mesatchee Creek Falls

Drive 7½ miles east from Chinook Pass on S.R. 410 to the turnoff at Wenatchee National Forest Road #1710. Park at the trailhead of

Union Creek Falls

Mesatchee Creek Trail #969 and begin hiking. After crossing Morse Creek and American River, the trail steepens considerably. The 100-foot falls can be seen from the trail after 1½ miles.

Union Creek Falls

Turn into the parking and picnic area at Union Creek Trail #956, located ten miles east of Chinook Pass. Follow the trail about one-fourth mile to a well-traveled, but unmarked spur leading to the 40 to 60-foot falls.

NACHES AREA

Drive to the junction of S.R. 410 and Little Naches Road #197, located 23½ miles east of Chinook Pass and 38 miles northwest of Yakima.

Horsetail Falls

This is a pretty falls during early spring and late autumn, but it becomes a trickle during the summer. Drive about three-fourths mile along Little Naches Road #197, then turn right (east) onto a short turnout. Water from an unnamed tributary descends 40 to 50 feet from cliffs into Little Naches River.

Devil Creek Falls

The unique geology of this area is not to be missed. Continue south on S.R. 410 for 3.3 miles beyond the Little Naches Road #197 junction. Follow the bridge across the Naches River and turn right (north) on Naches River Road #175. Park in 1.2 miles at Boulder Cave Picnic Area.

Hike an easy half mile along the canyon rim, then drop down to the base of these 20 to 30-foot falls. The falls alone would deserve a lower rating, but the bizarre landscape is also interesting. The waterfall is viewed from within a recess shaped like an amphitheater. Immediately downstream is Boulder Cave. At one time a landslide blocked the stream's course, but Devil Creek eventually eroded a tunnel through the debris. A flashlight is required to explore the cavern. A larger *Upper Falls* is 0.4 mile upstream, but there is no developed access.

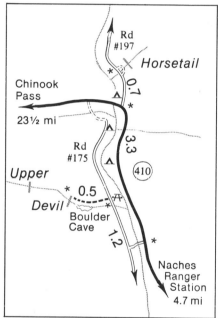

RIMROCK LAKE AREA

U.S. 12 traverses through the Rimrock Lake Area, a part of Wenatchee National Forest. The Tieton Ranger Station is a major reference point within the region. Drive 34 miles west from Yakima or 17 miles east from White Pass to arrive at the station.

South Fork Falls

Drive half a mile west of the ranger station, then turn south on Tieton Road #143. After 4½ miles, turn left (south) on South Fork Road #133. Continue for 11 miles, or one mile past the bridge over Bear Creek, to an undesignated parking turnout. Scramble a few yards down fishing access paths to the 20 to 30-foot falls along South Fork Tieton River.

Clear Lake Falls

Water tumbles along the drainage connecting Clear Lake with Rimrock Lake. Turn off U.S. 12 onto Tieton Road #143 ten miles west of the ranger station, or drive along the south side of Rimrock Lake via Road #143. From Road #143 turn on Clear Lake Road #1312. The waterfall is immediately upstream from the bridge over Clear Creek.

Clear Creek Falls

Drive 2½ miles east of White Pass along U.S. 12 to the marked parking area. Follow the trail a short ways along the canyon rim to a grand view of this spectacular 300-foot plunge along Clear Creek.

Upper Clear Creek Falls

Every waterfall collector should see this unusual configuration. One side of the 60 to 80-foot falls horsetails, while the other veils downward into a pool adjacent to the main portion of the creek. A trail a few yards upstream from the parking area leads to the descent.

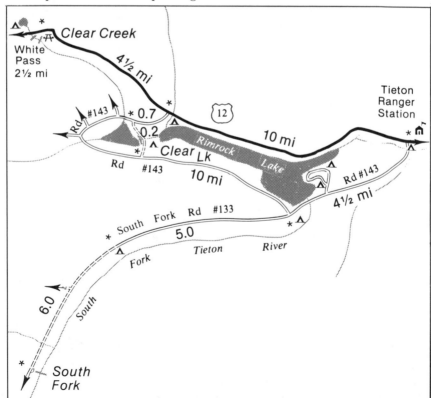

LOWER OHANAPECOSH DRAINAGE

Vacationers tend to zip past the northeast portion of Gifford Pinchot National Forest on their way to Mount Rainier during the summer and White Pass during the winter. Slow down. Better yet, stop and explore. The fine scenery includes, of course, waterfalls.

Lava Creek Falls

Drive on U.S. 12 to an obscurely marked turnout 7.6 miles west of White Pass and 4.8 miles east of the junction with S.R. 123. A vista overlooks the Clear Fork Cowlitz River canyon. Braids of water stream 200 to 250 feet down the facing canyon wall.

Upper Clear Creek Falls

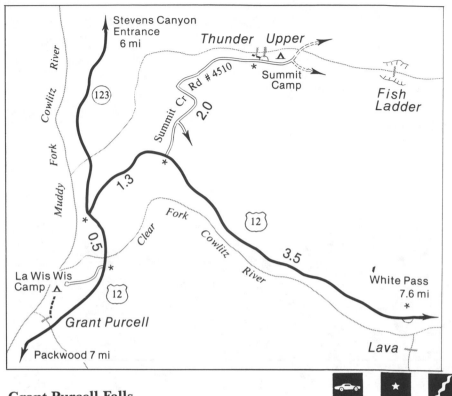

Grant Purcell Falls

Enter La Wis Wis Campground and park at the C-Loop Tent Site Area. A sign directs you to the trail leading shortly to Purcell Creek, which slides 75 to 100 feet across bedrock.

Upper Falls

Turn north on Summit Creek Road #4510 from U.S. 12. Two miles farther, park at the unmarked turnout on the north edge of the road. Follow the well-worn trail about 40 yards to Summit Creek and a view of rushing water skipping 25 to 35 feet across rock slabs.

Thunder Falls

Although a path leads to an excellent view of this 80-foot descent, the way is steep and recommended only for nimble hikers. Follow the trail down past the Upper Falls for almost one-fourth mile to the base of Thunder Falls.

Fish Ladder Falls

This entry has not been explored by a confirmed source, therefore I recommend it for experienced cross-country hikers only. Start at the bridge crossing at Summit Creek Camp and bushwhack along the stream for 1½ to two miles. **Do not** attempt an access farther upstream where Summit Creek Road #4510 runs adjacent to the falls. The creek is far below and the canyon walls are dangerously steep. The descent reportedly drops 150 feet along Summit Creek.

JOHNSON CREEK DRAINAGE

Rainbow Falls

This 100-foot drop from an unnamed tributary to Johnson Creek reduces to a trickle in late summer. Leave U.S. 12 at Skate Creek Road #52 across from Packwood Ranger Station. Turn right (northeast) onto Dixon Mountain Road #5260 in nine miles—just after Road #52 crosses Skate Creek for the second time. Drive 1.7 miles farther and park along the road. Scramble 100 yards up the small draw to the base of the falls.

SILVERBROOK AREA

Davis Creek Falls

Drive 5.7 miles east of Randle on U.S. 12, or ten miles west of Packwood to Davis Creek Road #63. In one mile, a bridge crosses 146 feet above the creek and its impressive gorge. Park across the bridge and find an unmarked trailhead about 20 yards from the span. The trail is extremely short, ending at the rim of the gorge with a view upstream toward the 30 to 50-foot falls. I've called this unnamed descent by the name of its stream.

Hopkins Creek Falls

Turn off U.S. 12 onto Silverbrook Road 5½ miles east of Randle or 11.2 miles west of Packwood. Park across the road from the first driveway to the right (east). The unmarked trailhead is obscured by vegetation. Search at the intersection of the road and the driveway. Once the trailhead is found, its well-worn path leads easily and quickly to the base of the 50 to 75-foot falls. I've called the descent by the name of the stream.

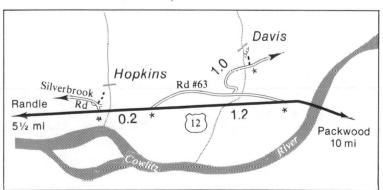

Panther Creek Falls

GIFFORD PINCHOT COUNTRY

Gifford Pinchot National Forest is named after the pioneer of professional forestry in the United States. Pinchot was the first chief of the U.S. Forest Service, serving under presidents McKinley, Roosevelt, and Taft from 1898 to 1910. During his tenure, the entire forest service system and administrative structure were developed. Pinchot's leadership in the conservation movement of this period was important in developing a policy of preserving and managing our nation's public lands.

There are at least 66 waterfalls in and about Gifford Pinchot National Forest. This chapter describes 38 of them. The recent volcanic activity at Mount St. Helens has had a significant impact on many of the region's waterfalls. *Harmony Falls,* which formerly fell 50 feet into Spirit Lake, was effectively destroyed by the catastrophic eruption of May 18, 1980.

The Iron Creek, North Fork Drainage, Cispus River Drainage, Kalama Falls, Eagle Cliff, and Lewis River areas described in this chapter are within the Mount St. Helens impact area. However, their descents were not altered to any measureable extent, but access has been restricted at various times from 1980 to 1982. At publication time, all of these areas were open to travel. I doubt that future volcanic activity of Mount St. Helens will significantly change the region over the next few decades. Rather, other volcanoes are coming overdue from their periods of dormancy. Mount Hood particularly merits watching.

COWLITZ RIVER

Cowlitz Falls

Leave U.S. 12 at Savio Road 2½ miles west of Randle and 13 miles east of Morton. Then turn on Kiona Road and drive 2½ miles south to Falls Road. Turn right (west) and drive six miles farther to a point where many spur roads join Falls Road. Continue south, then bear left (east) on a dirt road above the Cowlitz River. Park along a wide stretch of road about 0.9 mile from the maze of route intersections. Walk down the short, steep slope to the river. The 5 to 10-foot descent is visible from the rocky bank.

IRON CREEK

Iron Creek Falls

Turn off U.S. 12 about 1¼ miles west of Randle Ranger Station onto Randle-Lewis River Road #25. Drive about ten miles to Iron Creek Camp and continue ten additional miles along Road #25. The route rises far above the stream near the 60-foot falls. The descent is about half a mile past the junction to Big Creek Road #2517 and half a mile before Spirit Lake-Iron Creek Road #99.

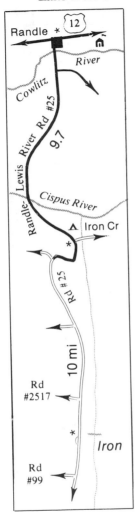

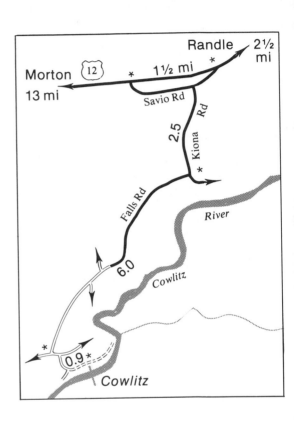

NORTH FORK DRAINAGE

There are two descents near North Fork Cispus River, but the flow of their waterfalls decreases as summer progresses. Turn off U.S. 12 on Randle-Lewis River Road #25 as to Iron Creek Falls, but after one mile, turn left (east) on Randle-Trout Lake Road #23. Drive 10½ miles, then bear left on North Fork Cispus Road #22. After 5.8 miles, turn off Road #22 to the right on Timonium Road #78.

Yozoo Creek Falls

Drive four miles along Timonium Road #78. The falls are on the right (south) side of the road.

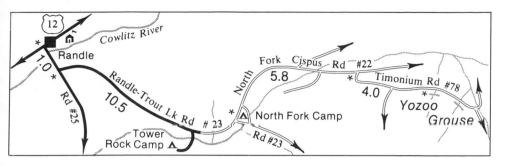

CISPUS RIVER DRAINAGE

Goat Creek Falls

Water breaks through boulders deposited by a former glacier, then
bounces 400 feet down a rock wall. Turn off U.S. 12 about three miles

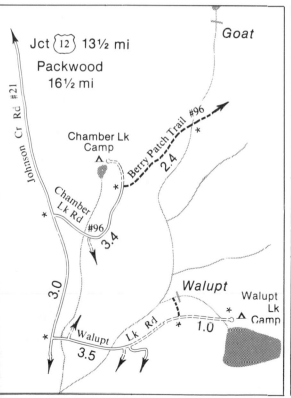

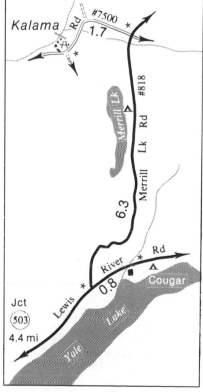

south of Packwood onto Johnson Creek Road #21. Drive 13½ miles south, then turn on Chambers Lake Road #2150. Continue 3.4 miles to Berry Patch Trail #96. Hike along this path for almost 2½ miles to Goat Creek. The falls can be seen 1½ to two miles upstream.

Walupt Creek Falls

Drive as to Goat Creek, but continue on Johnson Creek Road #21 three miles past Chambers Lake Road #2150. Turn left (east) on Walupt Lake Road #2160 and park at the guard station 3½ miles farther. Find the trail on the left (north) side of the road. The descent is about a quarter mile away.

Curly Creek Falls

KALAMA RIVER ROAD

Marietta Falls

Marietta Creek plunges and tumbles 75 to 100 feet into Kalama River. Exit Interstate 5 on Kalama River Road half a mile north of Kalama and drive four miles to the falls. Unfortunately, the only possible view is from the car window, since there are no parking turnouts. For better views, bring an inner tube or canoe and float down the main river. Launch your craft 0.4 mile upstream from the descent.

Lower Kalama River Falls

This 15 to 25-foot cascade is uninspiring, except when fish are swimming up it. Continue 4.4 miles past Marietta Falls to the marked turnoff to Kalama Falls Salmon Hatchery. The view is over the top of the falls at the end of the road.

LAKE MERWIN

Lake Merwin is the first of three reservoirs along Lewis River. The other two are Yale Lake and Swift Reservoir. The valley sides are steep, but two waterfalls are accessible. Turn off Interstate 5 at Woodland and drive east on S.R. 503.

Marble Creek Falls

Take S.R. 503 11.4 miles past Woodland to the Marble Creek bridge. Park at the turnout on the east side. Walk upstream through the lush meadow, then along a short footpath through a wooded tract. The 40 to 60-foot drop is less than 0.2 mile from the road. A lower falls is shown on the USGS topographic map, but apparently a rise in the reservoir's surface level has covered it.

Rock Creek Falls

Drive 6.2 miles past the previous entry and park on the east side of the Rock Creek bridge. When traffic is clear, walk across the interesting steel-girded span over the gorge. A couple hundred yards farther the 75 to 100-foot horsetail can be seen distantly across the canyon. The creek makes an unbelievable 180-degree bend around a rock outcrop near the falls. I have called this unnamed descent by the name of its stream.

KALAMA FALLS

Kalama Falls

Turn off Lewis River Road onto Merrill Lake Road #818 about 4.4 miles east of its junction with S.R. 503 and 0.8 mile west of Cougar. Drive north

6.3 miles, then turn left (west) on Road #7500. Continue 1¾ miles farther, as shown on the accompanying map. Park at any available turnout.

A short trail leads down to the Kalama River, then upstream to the base of the falls. The land is owned by the Weyerhaeuser Company. Trees blown down during the previous harsh winter made the path difficult to follow when I reviewed the falls.

EAGLE CLIFF AREA

The Eagle Cliff bridge over the Lewis River 19 miles east of Cougar marks the point of departure into yet another unpopulated segment of Gifford Pinchot National Forest. This bridge was reconstructed in 1981 after floodwaters from Mount St. Helens destroyed the previous span as a result of the major 1980 eruption.

Curly Creek Falls

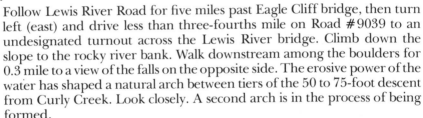

Follow Lewis River Road for five miles past Eagle Cliff bridge, then turn left (east) and drive less than three-fourths mile on Road #9039 to an undesignated turnout across the Lewis River bridge. Climb down the slope to the rocky river bank. Walk downstream among the boulders for 0.3 mile to a view of the falls on the opposite side. The erosive power of the water has shaped a natural arch between tiers of the 50 to 75-foot descent from Curly Creek. Look closely. A second arch is in the process of being formed.

Miller Creek Falls

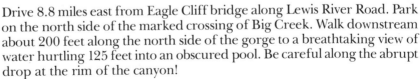

Continue 0.1 mile downstream from the previous descent to this 40 to 60-foot plunge on the other side of the Lewis River.

Big Creek Falls

Drive 8.8 miles east from Eagle Cliff bridge along Lewis River Road. Park on the north side of the marked crossing of Big Creek. Walk downstream about 200 feet along the north side of the gorge to a breathtaking view of water hurtling 125 feet into an obscured pool. Be careful along the abrupt drop at the rim of the canyon!

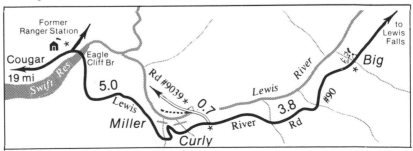

LEWIS RIVER

The scenic quality of the following falls within Gifford Pinchot National Forest tends to accentuate as you progress downstream. Therefore, the farthest entries have been listed first.

Straight Creek Falls

Drive to the parking area of Quartz Creek Trailhead #5, located next to Lewis River Road 16.8 miles northeast of Eagle Cliff bridge and eight miles past Big Creek. Hike two miles, passing a logged area in 1¾ miles. Walk across the log bridge over Straight Creek, then pick your own path upstream to a pleasant series of cascades totalling 30 to 60 feet.

Upper Lewis Falls

Upper Falls Trail turns off from Lewis River Road at a sign 0.8 mile southwest of Quartz Creek Trail #5. The path is moderately steep but only a quarter mile long. At the end, Lewis River thunders over a 35-foot escarpment. *Middle Lewis Falls* is only a mile downstream, but it can only be reached by a difficult cross-country trek.

Copper Creek Falls

The waterfall descends sharply 40 to 60 feet along Copper Creek. Drive 0.8 mile southwest of Upper Falls Trail to Copper Creek. Walk through the woods down the east side of the gorge. After almost 200 feet, look back into the waterfall, which is below the main road.

Lower Lewis Falls

Drive to the unmarked, undeveloped campground next to Lewis River Road. It is located 1.2 miles south of Copper Creek, 14 miles northwest of Eagle Cliff bridge, or 5.2 miles north of Big Creek. Park on the southeast portion of the looped spur road. A short trail leads to good vistas overlooking the falls. A heavy volume of water crashes 35 feet in an impressive block form.

EAST FORK LEWIS RIVER

Four small waterfalls tumble along East Fork Lewis River. Follow the marked route three miles from the town of Battle Ground to Battle Ground Lake State Park. Continue 2¾ miles northbound from the state park, passing the hamlet of Heisson, to Lucia Falls Road.

Lucia Falls

The park surrounding this 15 to 25-foot descent is privately developed. There is an admittance fee. Drive 2.4 miles east along Lucia Falls Road. Turn at the Lucia Falls Park and Cafe.

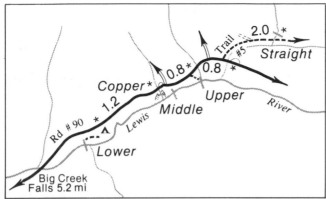

Upper Lewis Falls

Moulton Falls

Continue 3.2 miles past the above entry along Lucia Falls Road. Turn at the public park to views of East Fork Lewis River sliding 15 to 25 feet.

Horseshoe Falls

This crescent-shaped 20 to 30-foot descent would earn a higher rating if closer views were possible. Follow Lucia Falls Road to its end 0.3 mile past Moulton Falls. Take the right (southeast) fork called County Road # 12. This roadway rises 100 to 200 feet above the East Fork. Continue driving 4.6 miles to where the waterfall is visible from the road.

Sunset Falls

Drive three miles past the previous waterfall to Sunset Picnic Area. East Fork Lewis River splashes 20 feet a short way upstream.

DOUGAN CAMP

Dougan Falls

This stairstep series of block-type falls totals 30 to 50 feet along Washougal River. Water also slides 20 to 30 feet into the river from Dougan Creek. Turn off S.R. 14 onto S.R. 140 ten miles east of Washougal and 12 miles west of North Bonneville. Drive up the hill and after four miles, turn right (north) onto Washougal River Road. The waterfall is 7.2 miles farther where the road crosses the river for a second time.

BEACON ROCK STATE PARK

The 600-foot projection of Beacon Rock is a major landmark on the Washington side of the Columbia River Gorge. Nearby, Hamilton Mountain Trail passes two waterfalls. The State Park is next to S.R. 14 about 18 miles east of Washougal and four miles west of North Bonneville.

Hardy Falls

Turn off S.R. 14 onto the spur road across the highway from Beacon Rock. Drive 0.3 mile to the picnic area and the start of Hamilton Mountain Trail. After a moderate climb of about 1¼ miles, reach two short spur paths. The upper way to the far right leads to a viewpoint overlooking an 80 to 120-foot drop along Hardy Creek.

Rodney Falls

Hardy Creek plunges and cascades a total of 100 to 150 feet. Follow Hamilton Mountain trail as to Hardy Falls, but take the lower spur path to a viewpoint of the falls. Continue on the main trail to a footbridge crossing at the base of the falls. Another short spur ascends to the base of the upper portion.

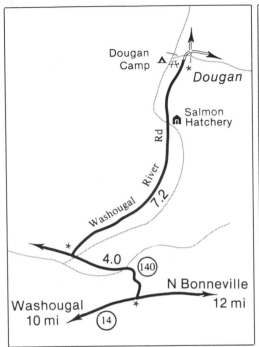

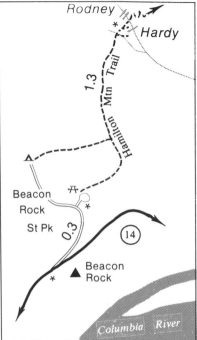

ROCK CREEK DRAINAGE

Rock Creek Falls

Turn off S.R. 14 onto Second Street either in Stevenson, or a mile west of town. Turn off Second street at Ryan Allen Road. In 0.2 mile, turn right on Iman Cemetery Road. Continue on this road to its end in 0.7 mile. A short, well-worn path leads shortly to side views of Rock Creek shimmering as it drops 35 to 50 feet over a wide ledge.

Steep Creek Falls

Go as to Rock Creek Falls, but instead of turning on Iman Cemetery Road, continue along Ryan Allen Road for one mile. Turn left (west) on Red Bluff Road and drive 5½ miles to where the gravel road crosses Rock Creek. Steep Creek can be seen tumbling 30 to 40 feet into the main creek. I have called this unnamed falls by the name of its stream.

CARSON AREA

The Carson area is best known for St. Martin Hot Springs, but the owners have periodically closed the waters to the public. Lesser-known Shipherd Falls, however, is always open to visitors.

Shipherd Falls

This 40 to 60-foot series of cascades along Wind River is next to a fishway, gauging station, and (locked) footbridge. Follow Hot Springs Avenue either from Carson or from S.R. 14 to Shipherd Springs Road. The gravelled route ends in 0.7 mile. A trail leads to views of the falls in 0.3 mile and 0.5 mile.

WIND RIVER ROAD

Panther Creek Falls

This 150 to 175-foot descent is unique because it is technically **two** waterfalls dropping side by side from Panther Creek and Big Creek! Turn onto

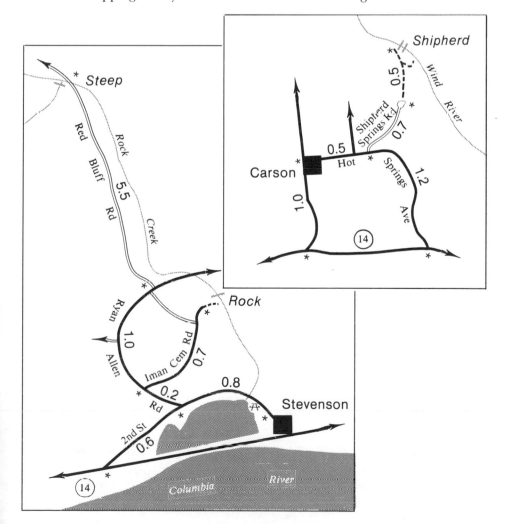

Wind River Road #30 from S.R. 14. Pass Carson in one mile and turn right (east) 5.8 miles farther on Old State Road. Almost immediately, take a left (north) onto Panther Creek Road #65. Drive 7.4 miles up this road and park across from its junction with Road #6511. Walk about 100 yards up Panther Creek Road #65 to a faint path which drops sharply down from the road (the most difficult part), then quickly leads to an undeveloped vista overlooking the falls.

Falls Creek Falls

This fantastic triple totaling 250 feet is so outstanding that I wonder why it has maintained such a common and dull name. Start on Wind River Road #30 as to *Panther Creek Falls,* but pass Old State Road and continue 9½ miles to Road #3062. Drive 2.3 miles on it to Lower Falls Creek Trail #152A.

The trail crosses Falls Creek in three-fourths mile. Half a mile beyond is a steep cascade, which can be forded easily during high water periods. The upper and middle portions of the falls come into view shortly. The trail ends in front of the middle and lower descents a quarter-mile farther. Superb!

DOG CREEK

Dog Creek Falls

Motorists zipping along S.R. 14 seldom notice this 15 to 25-foot waterfall. Stop at the undesignated parking area just west of mile marker 56, six miles east of Carson and ten miles west of Bingen. Walk a short distance upstream to the falls.

MOUNT ADAMS RANGER DISTRICT

The point of departure for the pleasing waterfalls of this area is Mount Adams District Ranger Station, located half a mile west of Trout Lake on S.R. 141.

Little Goose Creek Falls

Drive 9.3 miles northwest from the ranger station along Trout Lake Creek Road #88. Park on the northwest side of the gorge where the paved road leaves the creek. Although there is no trail, you can easily reach viewpoints looking down on the 75 to 100-foot triplet. Be careful at the canyon rim. The sheer cliffs are dangerously abrupt.

Langfield Falls

Continue 4.4 miles past the previous entry to the marked turnout for Langfield Falls. A short trail leads to an excellent viewpoint of Mosquito Creek veiling 110 feet downward. The waterfall is named after a retired ranger who apparently discovered it.

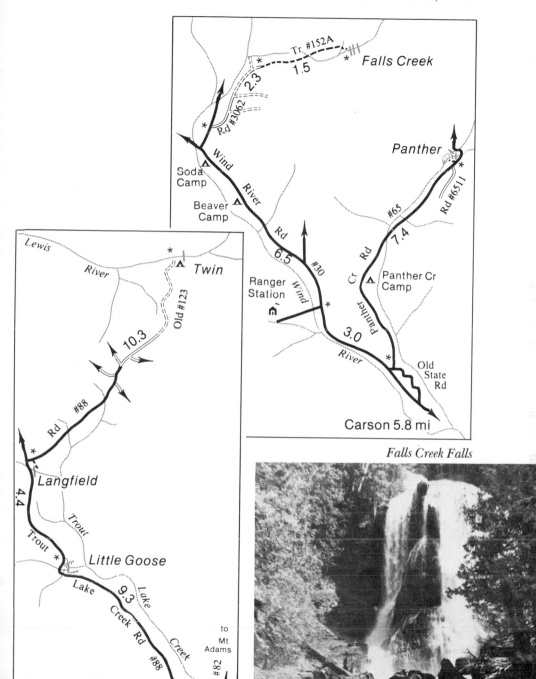

Tr #152A

1.5   *   Falls Creek

2.3

Rd #3062

*

Wind

Soda
Camp

Beaver
Camp

River

Rd

6.5

Wind

Ranger
Station

#30

River

Panther

Rd #6511

*

#65

7.4

Cr   Rd

Panther Cr
Camp

Panther

3.0

River

Old
State
Rd

Carson 5.8 mi

Falls Creek Falls

Lewis

River

Twin

Old #123

10.3

Rd   #88

*

Langfield

4.4

Trout

Trout

Little Goose

Lake

9.3

Lake

Creek

Creek   Rd

#88

to
Mt
Adams

King Rd #82

Trout Lake

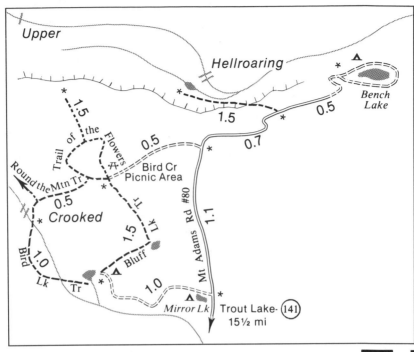

Twin Falls

Drive over ten miles past Langfield Falls to Lewis River. Trout Lake Creek Road #88 turns into gravelled Old Road #123 after five or six miles. The waterfall is upstream from the campground of the same name. It reportedly consists of a series of 2 to 10-foot descents. The best time to visit is from midsummer to midautumn.

MOUNT ADAMS WILDERNESS

These high country waterfalls are within the Yakima Indian Reservation and adjacent to Mount Adams Wilderness Area. The best visiting period is from late summer to early autumn.

Crooked Creek Falls

Proceed north from Trout Lake along King Road #82 for approximately 11 miles, then bear left (north) on Mount Adams Road #80. Drive 4½ miles to Mirror Lake. Using the accompanying map, choose your own trail through the meadows to the falls.

Upper Hellroaring Falls

Hike 1½ miles from Bird Creek Meadows Picnic Area to a vista overlooking the falls with Mount Adams in the background.

Hellroaring Falls

Drive to the junction of Mount Adams Road #80 and the access route to Bird Creek Picnic Area. Turn right (east) toward Bench Lake. Park at an overlook in three-fourths mile and find the trail descending into the valley. The trail ends at Heart Lake in 1½ miles. The waterfall is north along the next tributary. Due to the lack of information on this falls, I recommend it for cross-country hiking enthusiasts only.

GLENWOOD AREA

Outlet Falls

Outlet Creek roars toward Klickitat Canyon in an exciting 120 to 150-foot plunge. Drive to Glenwood from S.R. 141. The town is 20 miles from BZ Corner or 17 miles from Trout Lake. Continue six miles past Glenwood to the obscurely marked parking area and viewpoint. This canyon is unguarded and dangerously steep. Keep a close watch on youngsters.

Outlet Falls

Palouse Falls

THE INLAND EMPIRE

The eastern half of Washington is known locally as the Inland Empire. The name was popularized in the late 1800s when the region ceased to be part of the frontier. Since then it has grown into a substantial producer of agriculture products, timber, minerals, and hydroelectric power. Railroads played a vital role in developing the Inland Empire and establishing Spokane as its center of commerce. As a result, the region's rail passenger service is still known as "The Empire Builder."

The Inland Empire waterfalls were formed in two distinct areas by different geologic processes. North and northwest of Spokane are the Selkirk Mountains and the Okanogan Highlands. The Selkirks are composed of old sedimentary rocks ranging from 80 to 500 million years old. Recent folding and faulting, one to three million years ago, was followed by glaciation, giving the range its present appearance. The Okanogan Highlands, a complex metamorphic mixture of schists and gneisses, were formed and uplifted 50 to 75 million years ago. Glaciation and stream erosion have sharpened the peaks and valleys. Most of the falls in these mountainous terrains formed where rivers flow over heterogenous rock material. Escarpments are shaped where water descends from resistant rock to weaker components downstream.

The *Channeled Scablands,* west and southwest of Spokane, are a uniquely eroded province of the Columbia Plateau where waterfall development has paralleled scabland formation. Toward the end of the last Ice Age, 10,000 to 13,000 years ago, Glacial Lake Missoula occupied an area in western Montana roughly one-half the size of Lake Michigan. This glacial lake existed due to a natural ice dam which blocked the valley's drainage at Clark Fork in northern Idaho. The ice dam broke repeatedly, each time liberating staggering volumes of water to the Columbia Plateau and portions of the Palouse Hills. These events, called the *Spokane Floods,* scoured the landscape and created waterfalls from the Columbia and Snake River canyon rims.

Many of the cataracts are gone today, but the evidence of their magnitude is clearly visible. Famous *Dry Falls* was so powerful that its plunge pools remain, although 10,000 years have passed since its waters thundered over the adjacent rock walls!

The Spokane Floods also created a descent along Trail Lake Coulee called *Summer Falls.* It became a dry cataract once the floodwaters ceased, but the torrent has since been resurrected by an irrigation project whose outlet follows the coulee (stream bed). But don't procrastinate if you wish to see this waterfall. A new dam which would make *Summer Falls* dry again has been proposed.

The Palouse River originally flowed into the Columbia River, but the Spokane Floods diverted its course into a fracture in the basaltic bedrock near the present site of Washtucna. The new river course flowed south and eventually plunged into the Snake River. The waterfall has since eroded its way 7½ miles upstream, creating a 400 to 800-foot deep canyon from the Snake River to the present location of *Palouse Falls.*

SPOKANE

A renaissance occurred in downtown Spokane when the city hosted Expo '74, an international fair. The resulting national image boost has had a lasting effect. The former fair site is now Riverfront Park. It includes gardens, exhibits, an impressive Opera House, and several falls along the Spokane River. Turn off Interstate 90 at the U.S. 2/U.S. 395/Division Street exit. Turn north at the end of the ramp and drive eight blocks north to Spokane Falls Boulevard near Riverfront Park.

Spokane Falls

The Spokane River absolutely roars 60 to 100 feet downward as whitewater foams. An exciting gondola ride glides above the falls. When it is not operating, there is another good viewpoint near City Hall two blocks west of Riverfront Park.

Upper Falls

Walkway bridges cross close above 15 to 30-foot descents where Canada Island splits the Spokane River. There is also a vista at a small pavilion in the northwest corner of the park.

SPOKANE INDIAN RESERVATION

Don't bring your rod and reel to the following descents. Spokane Indian Reservation, like all Native American lands, prohibits public fishing in its streams.

Chamokane Falls

Turn off U.S. 2 at Reardan onto S.R. 231. Drive 13½ miles to Martha-Boardman Road, located about three-fourths mile past the bridge over Spokane River. Follow the dusty road 1.3 miles and bear right (north). After 0.7 mile, turn right on an old dirt road. Watch for an old sign attached to a tree at a turnoff 0.3 mile farther. Park at this junction and walk toward the creek. The road ends in half a mile at a small picnic site. Chamokane Creek tumbles 25 to 35 feet a short distance upstream.

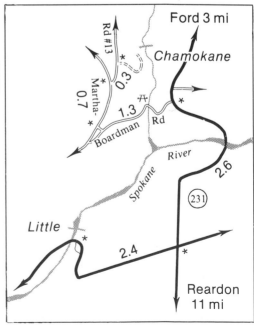

Pewee Falls

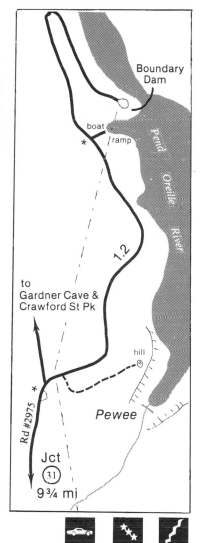

Little Falls

Spokane River pours off uniquely *V*-shaped Little Falls Dam, then cascades down another 20 to 30 feet. Turn off U.S. 2 at Reardan and drive 11 miles on S.R. 231 to the marked Little Falls access road. Drive 2.4 miles to the undesignated turnout on the east side of the river. There are good views from the bridge.

BOUNDARY DAM

This major descent is in the Colville National Forest in the northeastern tip of Washington. Additional attractions include Boundary Dam and Gardner Cave.

Pewee Falls

Pewee Creek ribbons 150 to 200 feet down a vertical rock wall into Boundary Dam Reservoir. This starkly beautiful waterfall was originally named *Periwee Falls* in 1895 by a French Canadian hunter and prospector. Turn off S.R. 31 onto Crawford Park Road #2975 south of the town of Metaline Falls. Boaters can drive 11 miles to the launch site preceding the dam. Follow the shoreline up the lake about 1½ miles to the falls.

A hilltop vista of the falls can be reached on foot, but I recommend it for experienced cross-country hikers only. Backtrack 1¼ miles from the boat ramp to an undesignated parking spot west of the powerlines. Walk up the road a short distance to avoid a marsh, then follow the powerline into the woods. After a few hundred yards, bear left (east) and climb the small knob 0.3 mile away. **Do not** attempt to get close to the descent, its stream, or the lakeside. Slopes in the drainage area are dangerously unstable and must be avoided.

PARK RAPIDS

Crystal Falls

Little Pend Oreille River descends a total of 60 to 80 feet in tiered fashion. Look for the marked turnout along S.R. 20, located 14 miles east of Colville and 22 miles southwest of Tiger ghost town. The waterfall is on privately owned land with public access.

COLVILLE AREA

The small city of Colville developed from old Fort Colville, a U.S. Army outpost from 1859 to 1882. There are two falls nearby.

Marble Creek Falls

Go east from Colville on S.R. 20 and turn left (north) on County Road #700 in 1¼ miles. After two miles, bear right on Alladin Road. Drive 11 miles farther, watching for the obscurely marked National Forest Road #200 to the left (west). Park along this primitive route, which soon deteriorates into a well-worn path. Marble Creek descends 25 to 35 feet a short distance farther.

Douglas Falls

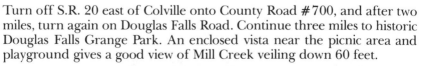

Turn off S.R. 20 east of Colville onto County Road #700, and after two miles, turn again on Douglas Falls Road. Continue three miles to historic Douglas Falls Grange Park. An enclosed vista near the picnic area and playground gives a good view of Mill Creek veiling down 60 feet.

In 1855, R.H. Douglas harnessed the cataract for a grist mill which he later converted into a sawmill. Failing to negotiate a lumber contract with Fort Colville, Douglas abandoned the project, but not his entrepreneurship. He turned his talents to the production of distilled spirits!

KETTLE FALLS

Kettle Falls is now only the name of a town. A cascade once tumbled nearby along the Columbia River, but the river's once mighty waters have since been pacified by Grand Coulee Dam, which created Franklin D. Roosevelt Lake. However, the area has two other descents.

Upper Falls

Turn off U.S. 395 and drive south through Kettle Falls. After three-fourths mile, turn left (south) on a paved road, then right on a dirt road

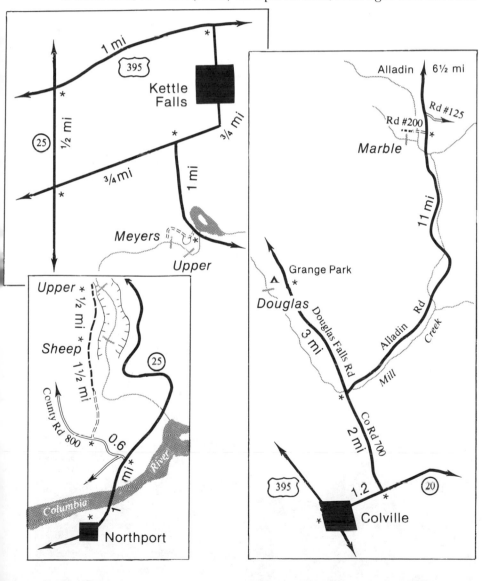

one mile farther. Park at the undesignated parking area and walk to the Colville River and this small 15 to 20-foot descent.

Meyers Falls

From Upper Falls, walk down the road a short distance to where the Colville River crashes 60 to 100 feet. Please respect the landowner's privacy by not driving on the road and by making your midday visit brief. The waterfall is named for Louther Walden Meyers, a pioneer who lived here in the 1860s. A small Washington Water Power facility now operates beneath the descent.

NORTHPORT

Sheep Creek Falls

Drive north along S.R. 25 to the village of Northport. Cross the Columbia River and turn left (west) on County Road #800. Continue approximately three-fourths mile to the first dirt road to the right (north). Park and hike along the primitive road about one mile to the canyon rim. Follow an old railroad grade for half a mile and look down on a high-volume cataract exploding 125 to 150 feet along Sheep Creek.

Upper Falls

Sheep Creek roars down 40 to 60 feet half a mile upstream from the main falls. The descent is a short distance below a collapsed railroad trestle, which marks the end of the trail.

CONCONULLY

Conconully is a small town 22 miles northwest of Omak in north-central Washington. One notable series of falls is accessible in this area.

Meyers Falls

Salmon Falls

Drive west from Conconully on Road #352. In 2½ miles turn right (north) on Road #364, then right again in 5½ miles on Road #3611. Continue a short distance farther to a marked turnout. The waterfall is not far from the trailhead, but the way is quite steep. West Fork Salmon Creek reportedly drops 300 feet in less than a quarter mile in four major descents.

COULEE CITY

Dry Falls

The largest waterfall ever known once plunged 400 feet over cliffs in five sweeping horseshoes totaling 3½ miles in width! The discharge was forty times mightier than Niagara Falls. Follow U.S. 2 west from Coulee City, turning south on S.R. 17. Stop at the scenic turnout and viewpoint two miles farther.

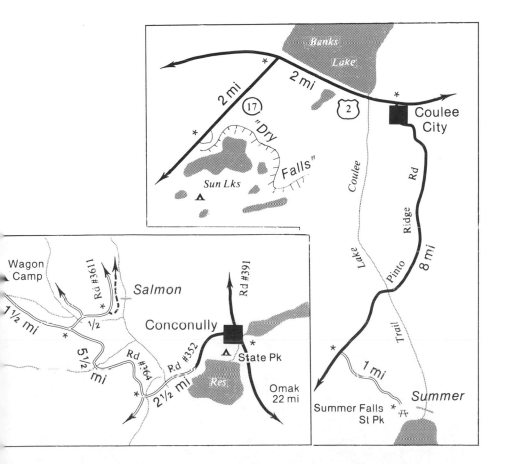

Summer Falls

Drive eight miles south of Coulee City along Pinto Ridge Road. Turn left (east) at the marked access road to Summer Falls State Park. The picnic area and falls are in one mile. The powerful outlet for Banks Lake Reservoir thunders 70 to 100 feet from Trail Lake Coulee. There is a memorial at the state park for three teenagers who, in 1978, drowned from the whirlpool action and forceful undertow in the basin beneath the falls.

ROCK CREEK COULEE

Rock Creek Falls

This cooling 10 to 15-foot drop in a sagebrush setting is located on private land. Fortunately, as the posted signs indicate, permission to hike can be obtained from the adjacent landowner. Drive along S.R. 23 about 1¼ miles west from Ewan. Find a dusty backroad to the left (south). Walk along this route for 1½ miles to the stream and the falls.

UPPER PALOUSE CANYON

Cattle rustlers still work in this area. The range land between the highway and the canyon is leased for grazing, so it is best to avoid suspicion by informing a county patrolman in Washtucna of your hiking plans.

Little Palouse Falls

At a 90-degree turn in the Palouse River, the stream widens to 200 feet and drops 15 feet as a solid sheet into a large circular basin. The river was diverted into a rock fracture here during the Spokane Floods. Drive along S.R. 26 east from Washtucna for 2.4 miles, or drive 6.6 miles west from Hooper. Park just west of the historical marker. Follow a dirt road 1.2 miles until it deteriorates into a trail above the falls. This route is a small portion of the historic Mullan Road which extended 624 miles between Fort Benton, Montana, and Walla Walla, Washington. Immigrants poured westward over it during the 1860s and 1870s.

Summer Falls

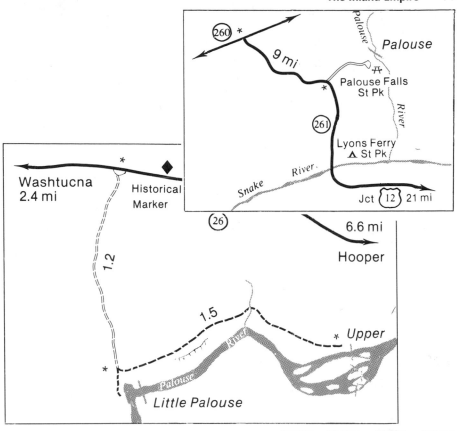

Upper Palouse Falls

The river separates into five different channels, each of which falls 22 feet. The descents are 1½ miles upstream from Little Palouse Falls. Hike along the canyon rim. The entry gets a low rating only because the view is poor from the north side of the river.

PALOUSE FALLS STATE PARK

Palouse Falls

Palouse River hurtles 185 feet into Lower Palouse Canyon in a thundering display. The formation of the falls is described in the introduction to this chapter. Turn off S.R. 260 onto S.R. 261 and drive nine miles southeast to the marked state park access road. To reach the falls from the south, turn onto S.R. 261 from U.S. 12 about 15 miles north of Dayton.

The Wilkes Expedition of 1841 called this descent *Aputapat Falls*. Unfortunately the name was later abandoned. In 1875 W.P. Breeding erected a flour mill at the falls. He envisioned a vibrant Palouse City at the site, but it never came to be.

Wahkeena Falls

THE COLUMBIA GORGE
OF OREGON

The Oregon side of the Columbia Gorge is a haven for waterfall lovers. Although it is the smallest of the 14 regions in this book, it has the greatest density of waterfalls. There are 71 recognized falls in this area of 420 square miles. Descriptions of 45 are given in this section. Ten additional falls should be accessible for viewing. The remaining 16 cannot be viewed either because no trails lead to them, or because they are in watersheds restricted to travel.

The majority of the falls along the Oregon side of the gorge were formed by the geological events which shaped the region. Two major lava flows occurred throughout much of the Pacific Northwest, one over 30 million years ago and the other about 15 million years ago. Although the mighty Columbia River was sometimes partially obstructed during these time periods, it always managed to erode through and resume its course to the Pacific Ocean.

As the layers of lava cooled, they predominately formed a rock type called basalt. The Cascade Mountains were formed by the uplifting of this bedrock material by internal earth forces. Most rivers were diverted by the creation of the Cascades because basalt is relatively resistant to erosion by running water. But the Columbia River was powerful enough to erode through the rising bedrock to shape the Columbia Gorge. The small streams which flow into the Columbia from the adjacent upland cannot effectively erode the basalt, so their courses are interrupted by the sharp, vertical breaks of the gorge and are seen as spectacular waterfalls.

These great waterfalls are limited to the south side of the gorge because landslides have modified the steepness of relief on the Washington side. The entire region's bedrock material is tilted slightly southward. When water-saturated, the upper basaltic layers on the north side of the river slide into the gorge. Therefore, descents on this side are smaller and fewer in number than in Oregon. The falls on the north side are described in the Gifford Pinchot chapter.

BRIDAL VEIL AREA

The Columbia Gorge Scenic Highway is accessible from Interstate 84 (formerly Interstate 80) for eastbounders at Troutdale (Exit 17), Lewis and Clark State Park (Exit 18), Corbett (Exit 22), or Bridal Veil (Exit 28). Westbounders get off at Dodson (Exit 35) or Warrendale (Exit 37).

Latourell Falls

This 249-foot waterfall along Latourell Creek is within Guy W. Talbot State Park. It is a short walk from the picnic area adjacent to the Scenic Highway to the viewpoint. The descent was named in August, 1887, after Joseph Latourell, a prominent settler in the locality.

Upper Latourell Falls

The trail to Latourell Falls continues moderately for 0.8 mile to the upper falls. Latourell Creek drops 75 to 100 feet. It is possible to walk behind the falling water. The park land was donated to the state of Oregon in 1929 by Mr. and Mrs. Guy W. Talbot.

Bridal Veil Falls

A short trail leading to this waterfall was under construction when this publication went to press. Bridal Veil Creek drops abruptly twice, the upper portion 60 to 100 feet and the lower portion 40 to 60 feet.

Coopey Falls

This waterfall drops 150 to 175 feet along Coopey Creek. For a view from above the falls, hike 0.6 mile up Angels Rest Trail #415 from the trailhead on the Scenic Highway. The descent is named for Charles Coopey, who owned the adjacent land. There is a convent near the base of the falls.

MULTNOMAH FALLS AREA

The following falls are accessible from the Columbia Gorge Scenic Highway, described previously for the Bridal Veil Area. In addition, the Multnomah Falls Rest Area (Exit 31) has a walkway to the vicinity.

Mist Falls

Water spirals down hundreds of feet from small Mist Creek. The falls can be viewed from the Scenic Highway 3.0 miles east of Bridal Veil and 0.8 mile west of Multnomah Falls near mile marker 19.

Wahkeena Falls

This 242-foot descent along Wahkeena Creek can be seen from the picnic area adjacent to the Scenic Highway. It was once known as *Gordan Falls,* but a committee appointed by the Mazamas, a regional association of outdoor recreationists, changed its name to Wahkeena in 1915. The name is a Yakima Indian word meaning "most beautiful."

Necktie Falls

This entry is accessible by a short side trail from the moderately steep Wahkeena Trail #420. The side trail is 0.8 mile from the trailhead at Wahkeena Falls picnic ground. The waterfall drops 30 to 50 feet along Wahkeena Creek.

Fairy Falls

Wahkeena Trail #420 crosses in front of the base of this 20 to 30-foot falls at Wahkeena Creek, about 0.3 mile past the side trail to Necktie Falls.

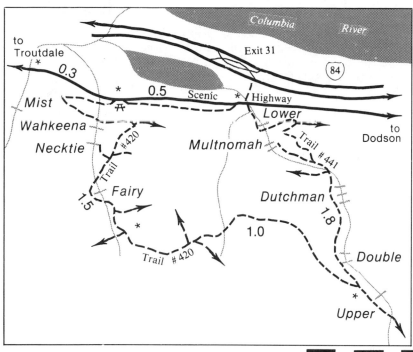

Multnomah Falls

The most famous waterfall of the Columbia Gorge is the fourth highest in the United States. The main portion of the falls plunges 542 feet while *Lower Multnomah Falls* drops 69 feet. Larch Mountain Trail #441 ascends steeply here. At the one-mile mark, a side trail leads to a viewpoint over Multnomah Falls. Upstream from the viewpoint is the 10 to 15-foot descent of *Little Multnomah Falls*.

Near the base of the lower falls Multnomah Falls Lodge houses a gift shop, restaurant, and visitor center. The following Indian folklore is told at the center:

"Many years ago, a terrible sickness came over the village of the Multnomah people and many died. An old medicine man of the tribe told the Chief of the Multnomahs that a pure and innocent maiden must go to a high cliff above the Big River and throw herself on the rocks below and the sickness would leave at once.

"The Chief did not want to ask any maiden to make the sacrifice. But, when the Chief's daughter saw the sickness on the face of her lover, she went to the high cliff and threw herself on the rocks below and the sickness went away.

"As a token of the maiden's welcome by the Great Spirit, a stream of water, silvery white, streamed over the cliff and broke into a floating mist along the face of the cliff. Even today, as you carefully watch, the maiden's face can be seen in the upper waterfall as the breeze gently rustles the watery strands of her silken hair."

Dutchman Falls

At this series of three falls along Multnomah Creek, the lower and upper falls drop 10 to 15 feet, while the middle descent tumbles 15 to 20 feet. The falls can be seen from Larch Mountain Trail #441 between 0.2 and 0.3 mile from the side trail to Multnomah Falls viewpoint.

Double Falls

Continue along Larch Mountain Trail #440 for 0.3 to 0.4 mile past Dutchman Falls to full views of the 50 to 75-foot lower falls and a view down from the top of the 100 to 125-foot upper falls.

Upper Multnomah Falls

This 15 to 20-foot drop can be viewed from Larch Mountain Trail #441 about 0.2 mile past Double Falls, near the junction with Wahkeena Trail #420.

ONEONTA AND HORSETAIL DRAINAGES

The cool, moist north-facing slopes and sheltered drainages of the Oregon side of the Columbia Gorge provides an environment for lush, diverse vegetation. This setting is described at Oneonta Gorge Botanical Area two miles east of Multnomah Falls along the Columbia Gorge Scenic Highway. The Bridal Veil Area Subsection describes accesses to the Scenic Highway.

Oneonta Falls

This descent drops 50 to 75 feet along Oneonta Creek. Hike up moderately strenuous Oneonta Trail #424 for 0.9 mile to its junction with Horsetail Falls Trail #438. Follow Trail #438 for a few hundred yards to the footbridge overlooking the falls. *Lower Oneonta Falls* can be heard but not seen from the trail. Reach the descent when the water is low by hiking upstream along Oneonta Gorge from the Botanical Area just off the Scenic Highway.

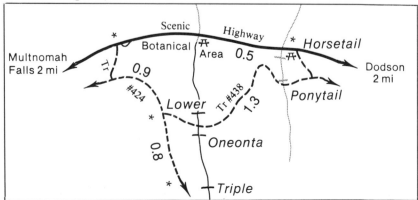

Triple Falls

Continue along Oneonta Trail #424 for 0.8 mile past the junction with Horsetail Falls Trail #438. The cataract plunges 100 to 135 feet along Oneonta Creek. It is of triplet form, not triple as the name implies.

Horsetail Falls

This 176-foot waterfall along Horsetail Creek can be viewed from a turnout from the Scenic Highway. It is a classic example of the horsetail form.

Ponytail Falls

These falls descend 100 to 125 feet along Horsetail Creek. They are 0.4 mile from the Scenic Highway along Horsetail Falls Trail #438. The trail goes behind the base of the falls. They are also referred to as *Upper Horsetail Falls.*

Triple Falls

JOHN B. YEON STATE PARK

The state park is adjacent to the east end of the Columbia Gorge Scenic Highway, just before it returns to Interstate 84.

Elowah Falls

McCord Creek plunges 289 feet within John B. Yeon State Park. For one viewpoint of the falls, climb the moderately steep Elowa Falls Trail for 0.8 mile. To reach the base of the falls, continue on Elowah Falls Trail, then turn on Gorge Trail #400 and follow it for 0.4 mile. A committee of the Mazamas, an outdoor recreation association, named the falls in 1915.

Upper McCord Creek Falls

Continue 0.2 mile past the upper viewpoint of Elowah Falls to these 100 to 125-foot falls.

Moffett Creek Falls

Hike 1.5 miles east past the McCord Creek bridge on Gorge Trail #400 to these falls. *Wahe Falls* is 0.2 mile farther upstream. I'm not sure whether a trail leads to this upper descent.

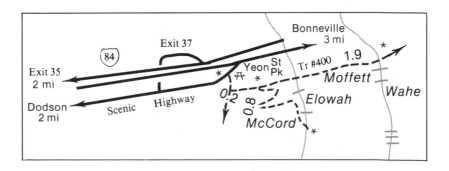

TANNER CREEK DRAINAGE

Wahclella Falls

Turn off Interstate 84 at Bonneville (Exit 40) and drive south to Tanner Creek Trail, which leads one mile to the base of the falls. It is a moderately steep climb and the trail is reported to be in poor condition. Also known as *Tanner Falls*, Wahclella Falls was named in 1915 by a committee of the Mazamas, an outdoor recreation association. Wahclella, the name of a nearby Indian locality, was chosen because of its pleasing sound. *East Fork Falls* is 0.2 mile and a 500-foot rise in elevation east of Wahclella Falls. No marked trail leads to this descent.

EAGLE CREEK DRAINAGE

Eastbound travelers can turn off at Eagle Creek Park (Exit 41), but westbound travelers must make a *U*-turn at Bonneville Dam (Exit 40) to reach

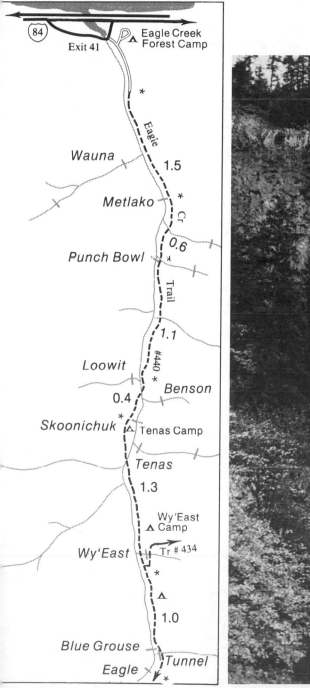

Multnomah Falls

Exit 41. They must make a similar turn at Cascade Locks (Exit 44) to get back westbound on the freeway. From the park, Eagle Creek Trail #440 ascends moderately 1,400 feet during its six-mile length.

Wauna Falls

This is the first of many descents along Eagle Creek Trail #440. *Wauna Falls* is on the first major tributary to Eagle Creek, about 1.1 miles from the trailhead. I've called these unnamed falls by the name of nearby Wauna Point.

Metlako Falls

This waterfall drops 100 to 150 feet along Eagle Creek. The viewpoint is 1.5 miles from the trailhead of Eagle Creek Trail #440. The descent was named for the legendary Indian goddess of the Salmon by a committee of the Mazamas, an outdoor recreation group, in 1915.

Punch Bowl Falls

Hike 0.6 mile past Metlako Falls viewpoint to a short side trail leading to the falls. Although descending only 10 to 15 feet, the waterfall is exquisite, a classic example of the punchbowl form.

Loowit Falls

This waterfall can be viewed across Eagle Creek toward Loowit Creek about 1.1 miles past the Punch Bowl Falls viewpoint. High Bridge crosses Eagle Creek a short distance farther, and soon after, *Benson Falls* is visible from the trail.

Skoonichuk Falls

This waterfall is along Eagle Creek, about 0.4 mile upstream from High Bridge. Tenas Camp is nearby and *Tenas Falls* are on a tributary 0.2 mile farther.

Wy'east Falls

From Tenas Camp, hike one mile to Wy'east Camp, then 0.3 mile farther to the junction of Eagle-Benson Trail #434. Wy'east Falls is a short walk down Trail #434. *Blue Grouse Falls* is on Eagle Creek Trail #440 about 1.2 miles past Wy'east Camp and 0.6 mile past Blue Grouse Camp. I've called both of these unnamed waterfalls after their nearby camps.

Tunnel Falls

Eagle Creek Trail #440 goes behind the base of Tunnel Falls at East Fork Eagle Creek 0.7 mile past Blue Grouse Camp. *Eagle Creek Falls* should be visible from Eagle Creek Trail #440 about 0.2 mile past Tunnel Falls. I felt I should call one of the previously unnamed falls within the drainage area by the name of the stream.

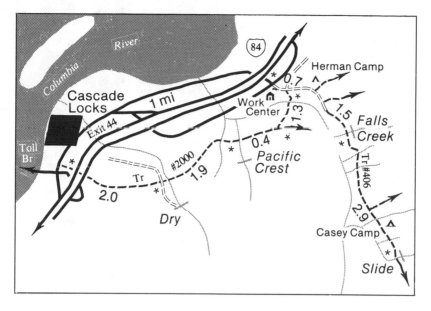

CASCADE LOCKS AREA

Turn off Interstate 84 at Cascade Locks (Exit 44). Access to this area's falls is via the Pacific Crest National Scenic Trail #2000. The northern Oregon portion of the trail begins at Bridge of the Gods. You can also start from the Columbia Gorge Work Center, located about one mile east of Cascade Locks. The trail is moderate to moderately steep for backpackers.

Dry Creek Falls

Starting from Bridge of the Gods, hike 2.0 miles along Pacific Crest Trail #2000 to Dry Creek. For those beginning from Columbia Gorge Work Center, hike 0.7 mile along Herman Creek Trail #406 to Herman Bridge Trail #406-E, then 1.3 miles to Pacific Crest Trail #2000. Follow Trail #2000 west 2.3 miles to Dry Creek. Once at Dry Creek, walk along the four-wheel drive road 0.4 mile upstream to the falls.

Pacific Crest Falls

This waterfall on a tributary to Herman Creek should be visible from Pacific Crest Trail #2000. The tributary is about 1.9 miles east of Dry Creek or 0.4 mile from the junction of Trail #2000 and Herman Bridge Trail #406-E. I've called this descent after the trail.

Falls Creek Falls

The descent can be viewed from Herman Creek Trail #406. It is 2.2 miles from the Columbia Gorge Work Center and 1.5 miles from the trail's junction with Herman Bridge Trail #406-E.

Slide Creek Falls

Visible from Herman Creek Trail #406, this descent is 2.9 miles past Falls Creek Falls.

STARVATION CREEK STATE PARK

Turn off Interstate 84 at the eastbound-only exit for Starvation Creek State Park and Rest Area (no camping). Westbounders must make a *U*-turn at Wyeth (Exit 51) to enter, then make a similar turn at Viento Park (Exit 56) when leaving. All of the following waterfalls can be glimpsed from Interstate 84.

Starvation Creek Falls

This 186-foot descent along Starvation Creek is a short distance from the picnic area. The name comes from an event in December 1884. Two trains of the recently completed railroad were snowbound nearby. The stranded passengers called the area "Starveout," although no one perished during the incident.

Cabin Creek Falls

Starting from Starvation Creek State Park, hike 0.3 mile along Mount Defiance Trail #413 to this 175 to 200-foot falls.

Hole in the Wall Falls

Walk 0.3 mile west from Cabin Creek Falls on Mount Defiance Trail #413. The 75 to 100-foot plunge once sprayed onto the highway, so the course of Warren Creek was diverted by blasting a tunnel through the adjacent basaltic cliff. The original descent was known as *Warren Falls*.

Lancaster Falls

Walk 0.2 mile past Hole in the Wall Falls along Mount Defiance Trail #413 to this 200 to 250-foot descent which falls seasonally along Wonder Creek. It was named in 1970 after Samuel C. Lancaster, who designed the beautiful Columbia River Scenic Highway prior to World War I.

Lindsey Creek Falls

Hike about 0.5 mile past Lancaster Falls, then instead of following the switchbacks up Mount Defiance Trail #413, bushwhack along the power-line for about 0.3 mile to Lindsey Creek. The descent is upstream about 0.5 mile and a 160-foot rise in elevation.

Summit Creek Falls

Continue along the powerline about 0.8 mile past Lindsey Creek to Summit Creek. The descent is upstream about 0.3 mile and a 240-foot rise in elevation.

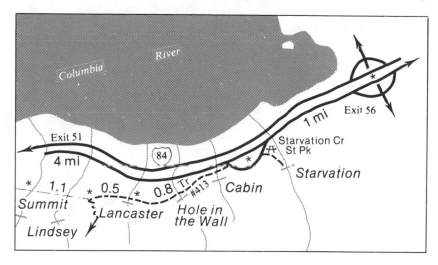

HOOD RIVER AREA

Drivers along Interstate 84 use Exits 62 and 64. The area can also be reached from the Mount Hood area on S.R. 35.

Wah Gwin Gwin Falls

This 207-foot plunge along Phelps Creek is on the grounds of the luxuriant Columbia Gorge Hotel. Leave I-84 at West Hood River/Westcliff Drive (Exit 62), turning left (west) at Westcliff Drive. The Hotel and falls are 0.2 mile away. Wah Gwin Gwin is an Indian word meaning "tumbling or rushing waters."

Punchbowl Falls

Drive to the town of Dee via a spur road from S.R. 35, then continue one mile north on Punchbowl Road to the falls along Dead Point Creek.

MOSIER AREA

Mosier Creek Falls

Turn off I-84 at Mosier (Exit 69). A short, easy trail on the right (east) side of Mosier Creek bridge leads to the 125 to 150-foot drop. I've called the waterfall by the name of its stream.

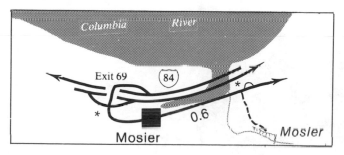

THE DALLES AREA

Turn off Interstate 84 at The Dalles East/U.S. 197 (Exit 87). Drive south 0.2 mile, then turn right (west) and go 0.2 mile to Southeast Frontage Road.

Cushing Falls

Drive one mile east along Southeast Frontage Road, then turn left and continue for 0.4 mile. Cross the bridge and turn right on an unimproved road. The 10 to 15-foot descent is a short, easy walk up Fifteenmile Creek.

Petersburg Falls

Continue for 2.5 miles on Southeast Frontage Road, then turn left and drive 0.4 mile on Fifteenmile Road. Park just before the bridge. The 5 to 10-foot cascades are a short walk away. I've called this unnamed descent by the place-name of the vicinity.

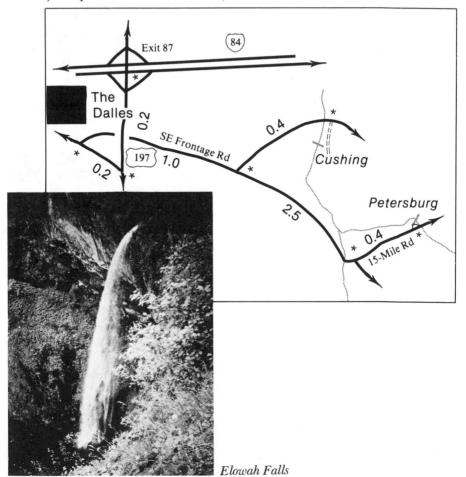

Elowah Falls

OREGON'S NORTH COAST RANGE

The Coast Range extends from the northwest lobe of Oregon southward to California. For convenience, the region has been divided into two chapters, entitled North Coast Range and South Coast Range. This chapter describes waterfalls found in association with the moist, montane environment stretching from the Columbia River, between Portland and Astoria, to an arbitrarily chosen southern limit along U.S. 20, connecting Newport and Corvallis.

During my travels along the coast, I found startling evidence that the Pacific Northwest has an enormous number of unmapped waterfalls. The northern Coast Range contains fewer mapped descents than most of the other regions of the northwest. The U.S. Geological survey topographic maps list 43, of which 14 are described in the following pages. But realistically many more falls occur in the area. Cal Baker of Hebo Ranger District in Siuslaw National Forest has surveyed and recorded 99 drops exceeding five feet—just in one district! Much of Idaho, Oregon, and Washington is more rugged and wild than the Coast Range, so if a similar proportion of falls are unlisted, the entire Northwest probably has over 10,000 falls in addition to the 700 currently mapped descents. It would require an encyclopedia-sized document to describe every waterfall!

SCAPPOOSE

Bonnie Falls

North Scappoose Creek tumbles 15 to 25 feet over a basalt escarpment. Turn off U.S. 30 at the north end of Scappoose and drive 4.3 miles northwest along Scappoose-Vernonia Road. A small parking turnout immediately precedes the falls. A fish ladder has been built next to the descent.

BEAVER CREEK

Motorists driving along U.S. 30 formerly passed two waterfalls between Rainier and Clatskanie, but the route was altered over a decade ago. Now few travelers see these descents unless they turn off the main route to look for them. Drive 6½ miles west from Rainier on U.S. 30 to the marked Delena turnoff 1.2 miles west of the turnoff to Vernonia.

Upper Falls

To reach this 10 to 15-foot cataract along Beaver Creek, turn off U.S. 30 onto Old Highway 30/Delena Road and drive 1.8 miles to the falls.

Beaver Falls

Continue 1.6 miles west from Upper Falls to an undesignated parking area to the left (south). Walk down the short dirt road to a path leading shortly to side views of water pouring 60 to 80 feet from Beaver Creek. Be careful. There are no guardrails around the viewpoint at the top of the descent.

OLNEY

Youngs River Falls

Drive ten miles southeast from Astoria on S.R. 202, or 20 miles northwest from Jewell. At Olney, turn south on the paved road marked Youngs River Falls. Continue four miles to the wide, unmarked parking area at a hairpin turn in the road. A short, easy trail leads to the base of the falls where Youngs River curtains 30 to 50 feet into the Klaskanine Valley.

JEWELL

Fishhawk Falls

Drive 4.4 miles northwest from Jewell along S.R. 202 to a marked picnic area. Trails lead upstream to the base of the falls in 0.2 mile. Fishhawk Creek ripples 40 to 60 feet downward. You can also drive 0.2 mile farther to an undesignated viewpoint above the falls.

Between Jewell and Fishhawk Falls is Jewell Meadows Wildlife Area. Elk and deer are often seen browsing in this state game refuge. There are marked viewpoints next to the highway.

NEHALEM RIVER ROAD

Two minor falls are found along the leisurely drive down winding Nehalem River Road. The road faithfully follows the meandering river for 27 miles through Tillamook State Forest between U.S. 26 and S.R. 53.

Little Falls

Turn off U.S. 26 near Elsie at the southbound turn marked Spruce Run County Park. Drive 5.2 miles to the park, then a mile farther to a sharp right (west) turn in both the road and the river. Park where the road widens. Fishing access paths lead to the falls where water cascades 5 to 10 feet over the 75 to 100-foot wide Nehalem River.

Nehalem Falls

Turn off U.S. 101 onto S.R. 53 near Wheeler. In 1.3 miles turn right (southeast) on Nehalem River Road and drive seven miles to the entrance to Nehalem Falls Park. Stop along the road about 100 yards inside the entrance. The Nehalem River slides 5 to 10 feet nearby.

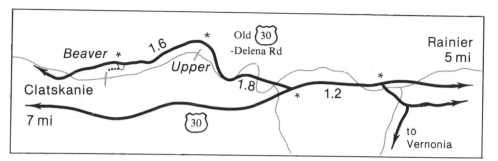

Beaver
1.6
*
Old (30)
-Delena Rd
Rainier
5 mi

Upper

Clatskanie
1.8
*
1.2

7 mi
(30)

to
Vernonia

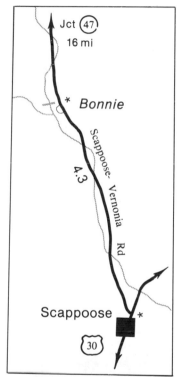

Jct (47)
16 mi

* Bonnie

Scappoose- Vernonia Rd

4.3

Scappoose
*

(30)

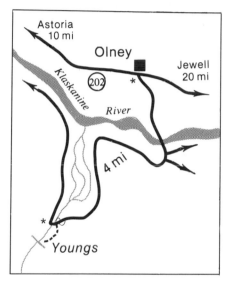

Astoria
10 mi

Olney

Jewell
20 mi

(202)
*

Klaskanine

River

4 mi

*
Youngs

Youngs River Falls

TILLAMOOK AREA

If this region's waterfalls have thus far left you uninspired, be patient. Buy some crackers and famous Tillamook cheese and drive to the following entry.

Munson Creek Falls

This fine-lined cataract dropping 266 feet is the highest waterfall in the Coast Range. Turn from U.S. 101 about halfway between Tillamook and Beaver at the sign for Munson Creek Falls County Park. Follow the signs 1.6 miles to the parking area and trailhead.

The easily hiked Lower Trail traverses through a lush forest to the base of the falls. For full views of the triple horsetail falls, follow the Upper Trail for half a mile to an excellent gorge vista. The trails were built as part of youth programs in 1960-62 and 1978-79. The waterfall is named for Goran Munson, who came from Michigan and settled along the creek in 1889.

Clarence Creek Falls

Turn off U.S. 101 at Beaver along the road marked Blaine. Drive 11.8 miles, then turn left (north) on Clarence Creek Road. The gravel route ascends steeply, then levels off to a gentle slope in 0.9 mile. Clarence Creek slides 45 feet adjacent to the road.

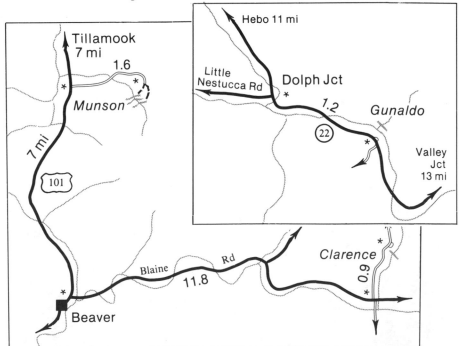

DOLPH

Gunaldo Falls

Drive toward Dolph junction, located where S.R. 22 and Little Nestucca River Road meet 11 miles south of Hebo and 14 miles northwest of Valley Junction. Take S.R. 22 from Dolph southeast for 1.2 miles to a wide expanse of the road immediately preceding a dirt road to the right (south). Listen for the falls. Scramble down the adjacent slope to the stream and continue to where an unnamed tributary sprays 65 feet into Sourgrass Creek 0.1 mile from the highway.

CHERRY GROVE

Cherry Grove is a small community nestled in the eastern foothills of the Coast Range. Two small waterfalls descend nearby along the refreshing waters of Tualatin River. Turn off S.R. 47 at Patton Valley Road six miles south of Forest Grove and 11 miles north of Yamhill. Drive six miles to the town, staying on the main road through the village. At a sweeping curve to the right, the route becomes Summit Avenue. Continue to the end of the paved surface and turn left (west) on a dirt road.

Little Lee Falls

Tualatin River splits into three parts before cascading 5 to 10 feet into a large pool. Drive along the dirt road past the scattered residential area into the forest to an unmarked turnout in 0.8 mile. The falls is a short walk away.

Lee Falls

Hike along the dirt road for an easy 1½ miles past Little Lee Falls to a gate blocking the way. Water pours 10 to 20 feet from a rocky escarpment adjacent to the road. *Haines Falls* is 1¾ miles farther upstream, but is not accessible.

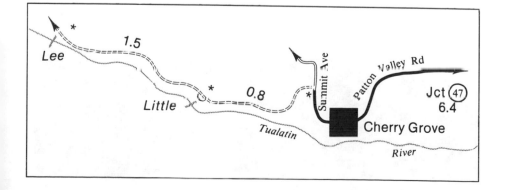

FALLS CITY

Falls City Falls

Little Luckiamute River sharply drops 25 to 35 feet into a tight gorge. To reach the community after which the waterfall is named, turn off S.R. 223 at the marked road six miles south of Dallas and 20 miles north of U.S. 20. Drive four miles to the town. Take the main road toward the west side of town. After crossing the river, turn right at the South Main Street sign and drive 0.1 mile to Michael Harding Park. There are side views of the falls from the park.

Falls City Falls

OREGON'S SOUTH COAST RANGE

The southern portion of Oregon's Coast Range extends from the north along S.R. 34, which connects Waldport and Corvallis, south to the California border, where the range is commonly called the Klamath Mountains. There are 33 waterfalls listed in this region; 23 of them are described here.

The landscape of the South Coast Range is geomorphically youthful. Its geology includes each of the three major classes of rocks. *Igneous* rocks, such as basalt, are common, as are *sedimentary* layers of sandstone and siltstone. Heat and pressure have transformed some of these rocks into the third category—*metamorphic* rocks. Gneiss and quartzite are examples. Each type of rock has a varying degree of resistance to erosion from running water.

This region once had a low relief, but internal earth forces uplifted and deformed the flat, coastal plains between one and three million years ago. The courses of most of the rivers flowing to the Pacific Ocean from the western flank of the Cascade Mountains were altered by this evolution of the Coast Range. Only two waterways, the Rogue River and the Umpqua River, were powerful enough to maintain their passages to the sea. Falls were shaped on these two rivers where rising bedrock with contrasting rates of erosion resistance met the stream beds.

Other major streams such as the Coquille River found new courses as the land surface rose. The rising bedrock of different forms also created waterfalls on these rivers. Additional descents formed where tributary creeks connected with larger rivers. As uplifting progressed, smaller streams generally eroded less effectively than the main channel. Therefore, a vertical drop is often seen near a tributary's confluence with the larger waterway. *Elk Creek Falls* is an example.

ALSEA AREA

Alsea on the eastern flank of the Coast Range is near two descents. The town is 25 miles southwest of Corvallis and 40 miles east of Tidewater on S.R. 34.

Fall Creek Falls

Fall Creek drops only 5 to 10 feet, but a fish ladder bypasses it. Follow S.R. 34 west of Alsea for 13 miles. Turn right (north) on Fall Creek Road. The waterfall is to the left in 1.2 miles.

Alsea Falls

South Fork Alsea Creek cascades 30 to 50 feet downward. Turn off S.R. 34 at Alsea and drive south for a mile. Then turn left (east) and continue 8.6 miles to Alsea Falls Picnic Area. This route is marked all the way from town. A short trail leads to the river and the falls.

SMITH RIVER

Smith River Falls

Turn off U.S. 101 onto Smith River Road, located north of Umpqua River and Reedsport. Drive 19 miles east, or eight miles past the junction with North Fork Road #48. The falls are to the right in a Bureau of Land Management picnic area. The river is named for Jedediah Strong Smith, an early 19th century fur trader and explorer.

MAPLETON RANGER DISTRICT

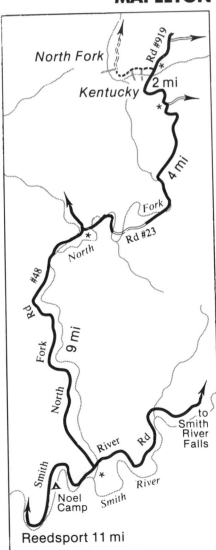

Following are the best falls within the Mapleton Ranger District of Siuslaw National Forest. At publication time, only an unimproved pathway passed next to these descents. However, the district was planning to construct a formal trail. Casual hikers should check with a ranger about the status of this project before starting into the backwoods. Ranger stations are located in Reedsport and Mapleton.

Drive 11 miles east of Reedsport along Smith River Road, then turn left (north) on North Fork Road #48. After nine miles, bear right (east) on Road #23. Follow this route four miles and bear left on Road #919. The trailhead is two miles farther on the north side of Kentucky Creek.

Upper Kentucky Falls

Follow the moderately descending trail for three-fourths mile to water veiling along Kentucky Creek.

Lower Kentucky Falls

Walk past the upper falls to this lower descent a short distance downstream.

North Fork Falls

Continue one mile past the lower falls to the North Fork. The waterfall is immediately upstream from where the river meets Kentucky Creek. Topographic maps suggest that the descent is 80 to 120 feet.

LORANE AREA

Siuslaw Falls

Water stairsteps 5 to 10 feet over a 70-foot wide expanse of Siuslaw River. Drive 13 miles northwest from Cottage Grove to the hamlet of Lorane. Continue west 8.8 miles to an unnamed county park. Stop half a mile down the park access road. The falls is a short walk away.

MILLICOMA RIVER DRAINAGE

Waterfalls are abundant on the various tributaries of Millicoma River. Unfortunately, most of them are inaccessible. But all is not lost. The most impressive falls of the area and indeed of the region are the center of attraction at Golden and Silver Falls State Park. Turn off U.S. 101 south of downtown Coos Bay, driving through Eastside and on to the logging community of Allegany in 14 miles. The state park is at the road's end ten miles farther.

Siuslaw Falls

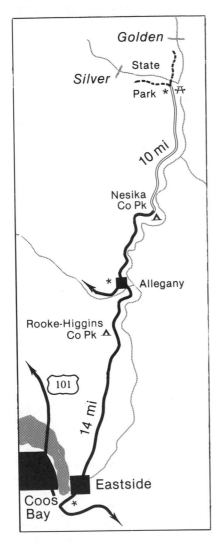

Golden Falls

Glenn Creek plummets 125 to 150 feet over a rock wall. Take the marked trail an easy quarter mile to the base of the falls. The descent is named after Dr. C.B. Golden, First Grand Chancellor of the Knights of Pythias of Oregon.

Silver Falls

Silver Creek trickles 80 to 120 feet over an unusual dome-shaped projection of weathered bedrock. Follow the second marked trail from the picnic area a quarter mile to the falls.

FAIRVIEW AREA

Laverne Falls

Leave S.R. 42 at Coquille and drive nine miles to Fairview. Continue north 5.6 miles past Fairview to popular Laverne County Park. The series of miniature falls, ranging from 3 to 5 feet, are near the camping area, downstream from the park entrance.

EAST FORK COQUILLE

There are many small waterfalls along the scenic East Fork Coquille River, and the historic Coos Bay Wagon Road follows beside it. Be careful when driving this narrow route. Logging trucks have replaced horse-drawn buggies! Be sure to find a safe place to park off the road when you locate each descent. Major accesses to this roadway are at Fairview from the west and Tenmile from the east.

Lower Falls

East Fork Coquille River tumbles 15 to 20 feet along a bend in the stream. The waterfall is 4½ miles east from Sitkum and 11 miles east of Dora.

Middle Falls

Water pours 15 to 20 feet over a small rock escarpment. Drive 0.6 mile upstream from Lower Falls.

Upper Falls

This low-lying 5 to 10 foot descent occurs where East Fork spreads downward next to a small, primitive campsite off the main road. The waterfall is 0.4 mile past the Middle Falls.

SISKIYOU NATIONAL FOREST

Siskiyou National Forest is a largely primitive portion of southwest Oregon's Coast Range. Many waterfalls here are currently inaccessible and unmapped. Also, seasonal descents are often seen along canyon roads during moist periods. Two of the most scenic cataracts are listed here.

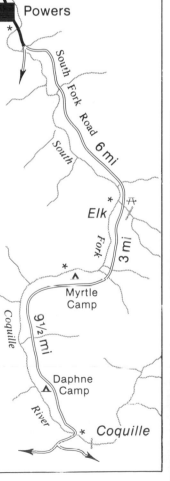

Elk Creek Falls

Elk Creek drops 75 feet over a rock bluff. Turn off S.R. 42 onto South Fork Coquille River Road three miles southeast of Myrtle Point. Drive 19 miles to the ranger station at Powers, then continue six miles south to Elk Creek Falls Picnic Ground. An easily hiked trail leads a quarter mile to the falls.

Golden Falls

Coquille River Falls

This backwoods location is recommended for experienced cross-country hikers only. Drive 12½ miles south of Elk Creek along Coquille River Road #33 to a bridge crossing the river. Bushwhack one mile upstream through the cedar forest to the base of the falls. Water sprays down 100 feet along South Fork Coquille River. The waterfall is in the undeveloped Coquille River Falls Natural Area.

ROGUE RIVER

The Rogue River cuts through the Klamath Mountains portion of the Coast Range, creating a 2,000-foot deep canyon. A 35-mile stretch of it is designated a *Wild River*, a federal classification intended to provide river recreation in a primitive setting and to preserve the natural, untamed integrity of the river and its surrounding environment. Such areas are generally accessible only by boat and trail.

An extended backpacking or float trip is essential to thoroughly enjoy the wild Rogue. The area should be studied before embarking upon such a journey. One excellent pamphlet is *The Wild and Scenic Rogue River*, published by the U.S. Forest Service and the Bureau of Land Management. Contact a ranger station or the Chamber of Commerce at Grants Pass or Gold Beach to get this and other publications about the Rogue.

Grave Creek Falls

Experienced whitewater adventurers negotiate this 5-foot chute without much difficulty. Drive seven miles north of Galice to the parking area past Grave Creek bridge. There are rapids next to the boat launch, and the falls 1,200 feet downstream.

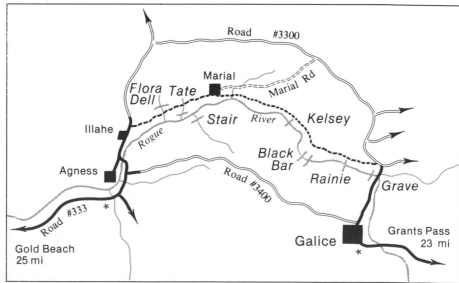

Rainie Falls

This is the largest descent along the Rogue. Because of its 10 to 15-foot drop, this cataract is too dangerous to run, but an adjacent fish ladder provides boaters an alternative to portaging. The waterfall is 1.3 miles downstream from Grave Creek Falls, Hikers can start at the parking area and walk 1.3 miles to a spur trail leading to the river and the falls. The escarpment formed because its highly resistant quartzite eroded at a slower rate than the bedrock immediately below.

Upper Black Bar Falls

Rogue River sharply drops a couple of feet downward 6.7 miles downstream from Rainie Falls. *Lower Black Bar Falls*, less severe than the upper falls, is 0.1 mile away. Neither descent is accessible by trail.

Kelsey Falls

To reach this minor series of cascades along the Rogue, float 5.4 miles past Lower Black Bar Falls. The descent is upstream from Kelsey Creek Camp.

Stair Creek Falls

This cataract tumbles from the side of the canyon into Rogue River. It is visible 2.3 miles downriver from Marial Lodge. The waterfall can also be seen from Inspiration Point, a trailside vista for hikers and backpackers 2.4 miles past Marial.

Tate Creek Falls

Tate Creek sprays 50 feet over sandstone into the Rogue River 6½ miles past Stair Creek, or two miles upstream from Flora Dell Creek. The trail passes above the falls.

Flora Dell Falls

Flora Dell Creek plunges 30 feet near the trail. Boaters can stop at the campsite two miles past Tate Creek. Backpackers hike ten miles west from Inspiration Point. Or they can hike 4.3 miles east from a trailhead on the gravel road to Illahe. The pool below the falls makes a good swimming hole.

MOUNT HOOD TO
MOUNT WASHINGTON

This chapter describes waterfalls from Mount Hood, located immediately south of the Columbia Gorge, through the Cascades to Mount Washington, 75 miles southward. Some sources have mentioned 76 descents in the vicinity. This book lists 43 of these cataracts.

The major peaks along the Cascades are actually volcanoes. The appearance of each mountain shows the relative time since it last experienced volcanic activity. The smooth slopes of Mount Hood (11,235 feet) indicates its youth, while Mount Jefferson (10,495 feet) is slightly older and hence more rugged. Three Fingered Jack (7,841 feet) and Mount Washington (7,802 feet) have very jagged features, suggesting that their volcanic activity ceased long ago and that lengthy glacial erosion has since greatly modified the once smooth form of these peaks.

Glaciation created the waterfalls associated with the volcanic mountains of the high Cascades. The alpine glaciers which top these peaks today once extended to lower elevations. Streams sometimes descend from adjacent walls into the valleys carved by glaciers. *Switchback Falls* is an example. Some cataracts are found on the valley floor where the glacier eroded unevenly, as at *Gatch Falls*, or where the present stream cuts over a highly resistant rock escarpment, as at *Downing Creek Falls*.

The many falls along the western flank of the Cascades formed in a manner related to the development of the range itself. About 20 to 30 million years ago, lava flows and accumulations of ashfalls alternatively covered the region. The lava hardened to become *basaltic* bedrock. The volcanic ash mixed with dust to create rock layers called *tuffaceous sandstone*. The area was uplifted and folded 12 million years ago, forming the Cascade Range.

As streams carved courses from the high Cascades westward, their flowing waters eroded the softer sandstone much more rapidly than the resistant basalt. At descents in Silver Falls State Park and from McKenzie River, water plunges over ledges of basalt. Recesses beneath the falls are open amphitheaters where sandstone layers have been eroded away by the running water.

MOUNT HOOD WILDERNESS

One of 12 wilderness areas in Oregon, Mount Hood Wilderness has over 35 square miles of pristine sanctuary just a few miles from metropolitan Portland.

Ramona Falls

Turn north off U.S. 26 onto Lolo Pass Road N12 at Zigzag. Bear right in 3¾ miles on Muddy Fork Road S25, driving to its end in four miles. Sandy River Trail #797 begins at the road's end. Hike two miles to where Sandy River veils 45 feet downward.

ZIGZAG RIVER DRAINAGE

Devil Canyon Falls

An unnamed stream within Devil Canyon reportedly plunges 50 to 75 feet. Drive about 1¼ miles southeast past Rhododendron along U.S. 26. Turn left (north) on Road #27. Follow its unimproved surface up Enola Hill. Park along the roadside when the route becomes too rough. The falls can be seen from a curve on this dirt road about 2½ to 3½ miles from the main highway. I've called the falls by the name of the canyon.

Yocum Falls

Drive along U.S. 26 to a Sno-Park wayside about seven miles east of Rhododendron and one mile west of the entrance to Ski-Bowl Resort. Look down from the parking area for a view of Camp Creek sliding down hundreds of feet. Mirror Lake Trailhead is immediately upstream. The waterfall is named after Oliver C. Yocum, who developed the vicinity's Government Camp hotel and resort in 1900.

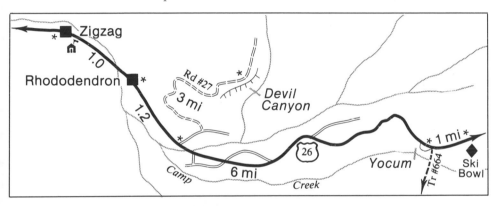

BENNETT PASS

Switchback Falls

North Fork Iron Creek cascades steeply 100 to 200 feet next to S.R. 35. The descent is aptly named for the winding path of the highway. Drive to the undesignated turnout one mile past Road S408 and 1.4 miles from the entrance to Mount Hood Meadows Ski Area. The falls is immediately above the road.

Sahalie Falls

Bright water tumbles 60 to 100 feet along East Fork Hood River. Turn at the entrance to Mount Hood Meadows Ski Area, then bear right on an old paved road. Stop near the bridge crossing in 0.4 miles. The falls is a short distance upstream. Sahalie is a Chinook word meaning "high." The falls was named by George Holman as part of a competition sponsored by the *Portland Telegram*.

Umbrella Falls

This 40 to 60-foot descent along East Fork Hood River is appropriately named. Drive 0.8 mile up the ski area access road to a sign marking Umbrella Falls Trail #667. Follow the trail 0.2 mile from the right (east) side of the road to the base of the falls.

Pencil Falls

Take Umbrella Falls Trail #667 from the left (west) side of the ski area road. Hike 1.3 miles to the trail's end at Timberline Trail #600. Turn right (northeast). Pass a ski lift on the way to the falls in half a mile.

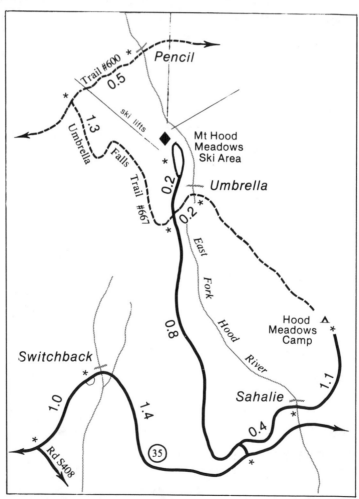

NORTHEAST MOUNT HOOD

Tamanawas Falls

Cold Spring Creek plunges 100 to 150 feet over a rock ledge in a deep woods setting.

Drive on S.R. 35 to Sherwood Campground nine miles north of Bennett Pass or 14 miles south of the town of Mount Hood. The parking area to the trail system is a quarter mile north of the camp. An easily hiked trail leads two miles to the falls. Tamanawas is a Chinook word for "friendly or guardian spirit."

Wallalute Falls

This waterfall reportedly roars down more than 100 feet along Eliot Branch. It can easily be seen from a roadside viewpoint. Turn off S.R. 35 onto Cooper Spur Road. In three miles, adjacent to the Cooper Spur Ski Area, turn right (northwest) on Cloud Cap Road S12. Follow this steeply graded, winding road to the viewpoint in nine to ten miles. Wallalute is a Wasco Indian term meaning "strong water." The falls was named in 1893 by Miss A.M. Long. She is believed to be the first white person to see the descent.

Tamanawas Falls

EAGLE CREEK

These two small waterfalls are not far from the Portland metropolitan area. Turn off S.R. 211 onto Southeast Eagle Creek Road, located 0.1 mile east of the junction with S.R. 224. Turn left (east) from Eagle Creek Road onto Southeast Wildcat Road, then bear right (south) on County Road #40.

The Falls

Drive 1.8 miles along County Road #40 to a yellow-gated turnout to the right. Eagle Creek descends 20 to 30 feet a short walk down a well-worn path from the turnout.

Eagle Creek Falls

Continue 2.7 miles past the previous descent on County Road #20. Park at the yellow-gated road to the right (south). Walk along the dirt road for 0.8 mile until the falls is heard. A short path leads to the base of a 20 to 30-foot block-type waterfall. Fishing is prohibited. I've called the falls by the name of its stream.

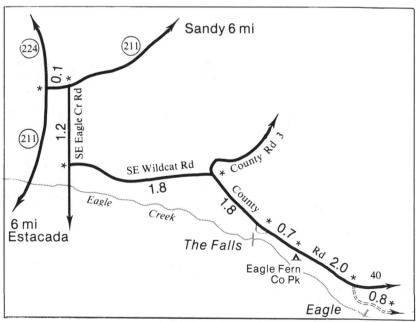

SOLITUDE

Pegleg Falls

Drive 25 miles southeast from Estacada on S.R. 224 to Clackamas River Road #46, half a mile past Ripplebrook Ranger Station. Four miles farther, turn right (south) on Collawash River Road #63. Continue another 3½ miles, then turn right onto Road S70. Drive seven miles to where Hot Springs Fork drops 35 feet. A fish ladder bypasses the waterfall.

South Falls

SILVER FALLS STATE PARK

This is a paradise for waterfall seekers. Silver Creek Canyon has ten major descents, all of them within moderate walking distances of the main highway. S.R. 214 goes through the park 14 miles southeast of Silverton and 25 miles east of Salem.

Upper North Falls

North Silver Creek drops 65 feet. Find the trail from the south side of the parking lot at the east end of the park. Cross under the highway and walk 0.3 mile to the descent.

North Falls

Take the previously mentioned trail 0.3 mile west to exciting views beside and behind this impressive 136-foot waterfall.

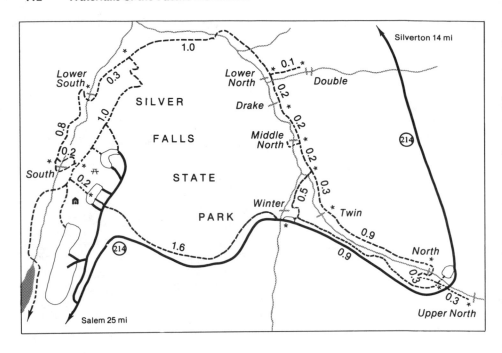

Twin Falls

North Silver Creek diverges in two streams as it tumbles 31 feet over weathered bedrock. Follow the trail 0.9 mile downstream from North Falls.

Middle North Falls

This unique waterfall hurtles through the air for two-thirds of its 106-foot drop, then veils over bedrock for the final portion. Walk half a mile past Twin Falls or 0.7 miles past Winter Falls (described later) to view this entry. A side trail goes behind and around the descent.

Drake Falls

Hike 0.2 mile downstream from Middle North Falls to this 27-foot curtain of water.

Double Falls

Water drops a total of 178 feet in tiered form. The lower portion descends four times as far than the upper part. Walk 0.3 mile past Drake Falls to the spur trail at Hullt Creek.

Lower North Falls

This 30-foot drop is immediately downstream from the mouth of Hullt Creek along North Silver Creek.

Winter Falls

Winter Creek falls 134 feet in two forms. Initially it plunges down, then becomes a horsetail. Walk a short distance from the designated turnout on S.R. 214, as shown on the accompanying map.

South Falls

This is the highlight of the park. South Silver Creek drops 177 feet over a ledge of basalt. Walk about 0.4 mile from the parking areas. Vistas and trailsides reveal the many faces of the falls. There is a lodge and gift shop between the main parking area and South Falls.

Lower South Falls

The trail passes behind this 93-foot descent located 0.8 mile downstream from South Falls.

MEHAMA

This area has three falls located on Bureau of Land Management parcels. Turn off S.R. 22 north onto Fenn Ridge Road at Mehama. Drive uphill 1.2 miles, then take a sharp right (east) turn onto a gated gravel road. You can drive beyond the gate, but be sure to close it so the grazing livestock doesn't wander.

Stasel Falls

This 100 to 125-foot descent along Stout Creek would deserve a higher rating, but the side view is partially obstructed. Drive 1.6 miles from Fenn Ridge Road, parking next to a dirt road junction. Follow this unimproved route about 100 yards to paths leading to the top of abrupt cliffs and obstructed views upstream to the falls.

Lower Shellburg Falls

Backtrack 0.2 miles from the previous entry and park near Shellburg Creek and its lower 20 to 40-foot falls.

Shellburg Falls

This 80 to 100-foot plume descends over an extension of basalt along Shellburg Creek. Find the unmarked trail on the north side of the Bureau of Land Management road. The easily hiked trail goes behind the base of this descent in 0.2 mile.

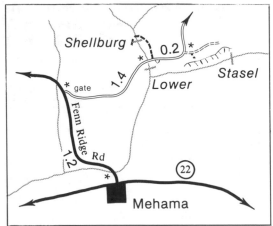

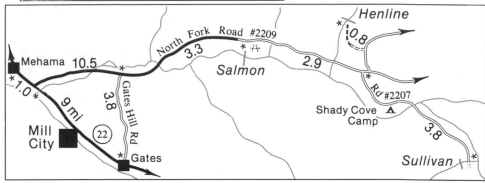

NORTH FORK DRAINAGE

Access to the pleasant Elkhorn Valley and waterfalls upstream is easiest via North Fork Road from S.R. 22 one mile east of Mehama. Alternatively, adventurous drivers with a reliable vehicle may wish to tackle Gates Hill Road. This gravel route travels up, up, up, then down, down, down from Gates to Elkhorn Valley.

Salmon Falls

A high volume 25 to 35-foot descent drops down along Little North Santiam River. Drive 3.3 miles up the valley from the junction of Gates Hill Road and North Fork Road #2209. Turn at the sign for Salmon Falls County Park. A fish ladder bypasses the cataract.

Henline Falls

Henline Creek falls 75 to 100 feet over a mountainside. Continue past Salmon Falls for 2.9 miles, then bear left 0.1 mile along Road #2209. Park and walk up the tributary road to the left. After about half a mile, turn left onto a dirt road which quickly becomes a well-worn trail. The falls is reached in a quarter mile. There is an interesting old mine shaft near the base of the descent. Look but don't enter!

Sullivan Creek Falls

This steep 40 to 60-foot cascade would deserve a higher rating, but the surrounding clear-cut land detracts from the scene. Turn right off Road #2209 onto Road #2207 about 2.9 miles past Salmon Falls. Drive along this gravel road 3.8 miles to the falls directly above a bridge over Sullivan Creek. I've called this unnamed descent by the name of its stream.

NIAGARA PARK

Niagara Park was the site of a small town from 1890 to 1934. A rubble masonry dam was built in the late 1890s to provide power for a paper mill. Difficulties in constructing the dam caused the mill project to be abandoned and the village faded. Historic remnants of the town can be seen at a marked turnout 4.2 miles east of Gates and 13 miles west of Detroit along S.R. 22.

Sevenmile Creek Falls

Walk down a trail and scramble on interesting rock formations to view this descent from across North Santiam River. I've called it by the name of the stream.

MARION FORKS AREA

Whispering Falls

Misery Creek falls 40 to 60 feet into North Santiam River. Drive to Whispering Falls Campground, located on S.R. 22 four miles east of Idanha. The waterfall is across the river from the camp. Probably it got its name from the fact that the busy North Santiam drowns out the sound of the falls.

Gatch Falls

This beautiful 75 to 100-foot waterfall from Marion Creek is also known as *Gooch Falls*. Turn off S.R. 22 at Marion Forks onto Marion Creek Road #2255. Follow the gravel road for 3½ miles, then turn right on Road #2255/850. Park where the dirt road widens in less than 0.2 mile. Walk carefully toward the creek for a natural, unfenced view above and into the falls.

Downing Creek Falls

Drive 3.4 miles south from Marion Forks on S.R. 22 to an undesignated turnout and camping site on the left (east) side of the highway. Walk a short distance upstream to where Downing Creek flows 20 to 30 feet down a chute. I've called the descent by the name of the stream.

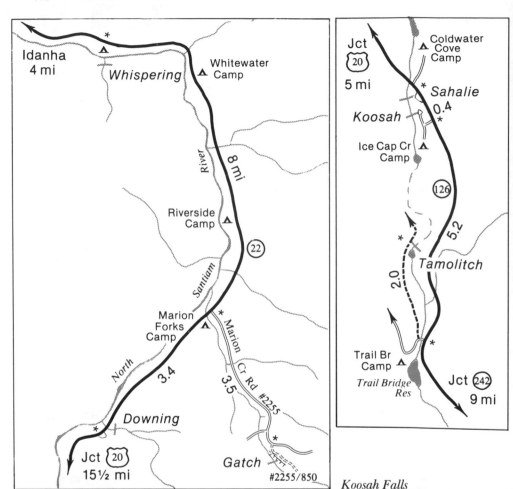

Idanha
4 mi

Whispering

Whitewater
Camp

River

8 mi

Riverside
Camp

Santiam

22

Marion
Forks
Camp

Marion Cr Rd #2255

North

3.4

3.5

Downing

Jct 20
15½ mi

Gatch

#2255/850

Jct 20
5 mi

Coldwater
Cove
Camp

Sahalie
0.4

Koosah

Ice Cap Cr
Camp

126

5.2

2.0

Tamolitch

Trail Br
Camp

*Trail Bridge
Res*

Jct 242
9 mi

Koosah Falls

McKENZIE RIVER

The waterfalls along the McKenzie River descend with fury, except Tamolitch which has been artificially turned off.

Sahalie Falls

This roaring 140-foot torrent can be seen from developed viewpoints. Turn at the point of interest sign along S.R. 126 located 5.2 miles south of U.S. 20 and six miles north of Belknap Springs. Sahalie is a Chinook word meaning "high."

Koosah Falls

McKenzie River thunders 80 to 120 feet over a sharp escarpment. Drive 0.4 mile south of the previous descent along S.R. 126 to the entrance marked Ice Cap Campground. The parking area and developed viewpoints are in 0.3 mile.

Tamolitch Falls

A 60-foot dry rock wall is the only thing left where water once poured from McKenzie River. But by all means, visit this location! Turn off S.R. 126 at the north end of Trail Bridge Reservoir half a mile north of Belknap Springs, or 5.2 miles south of Koosah Falls. Drive about three-fourths mile to the McKenzie River Trailhead.

Hike up the trail along the river for two miles to a crystal clear, cyan-colored pool with the dry falls at its head. This circular basin inspired the name Tamolitch, which is Chinook for "tub" or "bucket." At this site, you will see a very rare phenomenon—a full-sized river beginning at a single point. Springs feed the plunge pool at the base of the dry cataract. Superb!

What happened to the falls? The river has been diverted three miles upstream at Carmen Reservoir. A tunnel directs the water to Smith Reservoir and the power generating facilities in the adjacent drainage area.

CASCADIA

Lower Soda Creek Falls

Soda Creek tumbles 150 to 180 feet in three tiers among moss-covered rocks. Start at Cascadia State Park 13 miles east of Sweet Home near U.S. 20. Find the unmarked trail at the far north end of the campsite and hike a moderate half mile to the falls.

Rainbow Falls

Drive 0.9 mile east from Cascadia, turning right (south) from U.S. 20 on Swamp Mountain Road. Follow up this gravel route for 1.7 miles, parking

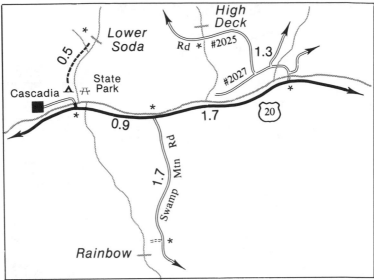

at an old dirt road to the right. Follow it for about 100 feet, then descend to a small ridge from which you can see Dobbin Creek pouring 20 to 30 feet into a pool.

High Deck Falls

Water cascades steeply for more than 100 feet along an unnamed creek. Continue along U.S. 20 for 1.7 miles past Swamp Mountain Road to Moose Creek Road #2027. Follow the turns as shown on the accompanying map to Road #2025 and the falls in 1.3 miles. I've called the descent by the name of the nearby mountain.

McDOWELL FALLS AREA

Four of the five waterfalls described in the subsection are within McDowell Creek Falls County Park, a pleasant and thoughtfully planned day-use recreation area. Turn off U.S. 20 at Fairview Road. Turn left, then right onto McDowell Creek Road in one mile. The county park and first parking turnout are in 7½ miles.

Lower Falls

This minor pair of 5 to 10-foot drops along McDowell Creek is located immediately downstream from the footbridge at the southern beginning of the trail.

Royal Terrace Falls

Fall Creek sprays 119 feet down in a fountainlike tiered display. Walk an easy 0.3 mile upstream from Lower Falls to this waterfall. A marked spur path goes to a viewpoint from the top of the cataract.

Majestic Falls

A porchlike overlook allows a close-up view of this 30 to 40-foot drop tumbling from McDowell Creek. Drive to the north end of the park. A stairway leads shortly to the vista.

Crystal Falls

McDowell Creek skips 10 to 15 feet into punchbowl-shaped Crystal Pool. Continue 0.1 mile past Majestic Falls to an overview of this waterfall.

Coal Creek Falls

Reach Green Peter Dam Road from McDowell Falls Park via Sunnyside Drive, or from U.S. 20 at the east end of Foster Lake. Once you come alongside Middle Santiam River, drive east 1.6 miles and park at the dirt road to the left (north). Walk to the end of the road, then scramble up the crumbly slope to a faint path. A short distance farther you can see the 40 to 60-foot drop. The walk totals a quarter mile. I've called this descent by the name of its stream.

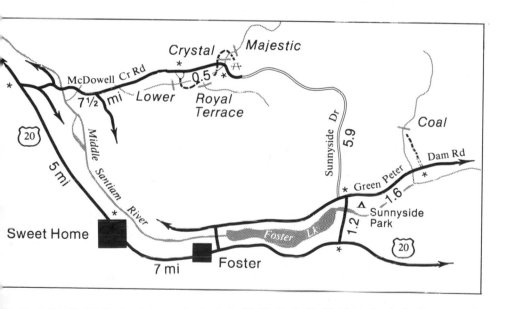

THE SOUTH CASCADES OF OREGON

South-central Oregon presents a collage of scenic outdoor settings typical of the Cascade Range. The area's major peaks include Three Sisters, Bachelor Butte, Diamond Peak, and Mount McLoughlin—all of them volcanic in origin. The region also boasts five national forests, four wilderness areas, an abundance of mountain lakes, and Crater Lake National Park.

Waterfalls are well-distributed throughout the South Cascades. Most of the 53 recognized descents in the region are relatively accessible; 43 of them are listed in this book. Many are among the most majestic in the Pacific Northwest.

Falls are commonly found streaming down canyon walls carved by alpine glaciers. During the last major Ice Age, 10,000 to 14,000 years ago, these glaciers extended their range to areas below 2,500 feet in elevation in the South Cascades. Large, *U*-shaped *glacial troughs* remain as evidence of the intense erosive powers of these glaciers. Today, rivers follow the valleys abandoned by the retreating glaciers. As tributary streams flow into the troughs, they often drop sharply as waterfalls. *Rainbow Falls, Proxy Falls,* and *Vidae Falls* are examples. Many physical geographers and geologists refer to this type of descent as *ribbon falls.*

The western portion of the South Cascades formed in the same manner as the north extension described in the preceding chapter. Where layers of resistant basalt and weak sandstone meet along a stream's course, the sandstone erodes faster than the basalt. The graceful *Toketee Falls* and *Grotto Falls* are good examples of cataracts shaped in this way.

THREE SISTERS WILDERNESS

The peaks of North Sister (10,085 feet), Middle Sister (10,047 feet), and South Sister (10,358 feet) dominate the Cascade scenery along S.R. 242. The major waterfalls of this wilderness area are easily accessible.

Rainbow Falls

Turn off S.R. 126 onto Foley Ridge Road #2643 about half a mile east of McKenzie Bridge Ranger Station. Follow Road #2643 for 6.4 miles, then turn right on the marked dirt road to the start of Rainbow Falls Trail #3543. The moderately easy trail ends in three-fourths mile at the unfenced viewpoint. Rainbow Creek can be seen descending 150 to 200 feet on the other side of the valley with Three Sisters in the background.

Upper Falls

Water steeply cascades 100 to 125 feet from springs issuing from a high canyon wall. Turn off S.R. 126 onto S.R. 242 and drive 6.3 miles east to the

Proxy Falls

turnout for Proxy Falls Trail #3532. Hike about half a mile, then take a left fork to the Upper Falls.

Proxy Falls

Proxy Creek pours 200 feet in impressive fashion. Follow the right spur of Trail #3532, labeled Lower Falls. It leads shortly to a developed viewpoint overlooking the falls.

CASCADE LAKES HIGHWAY

Fall Creek Falls

Drive west from Bend for 28 miles on the Cascade Lakes Highway, also known as Century Drive. Turn at the marked access road for Green Lakes Trail #17, located on the west side of Fall Creek. Drive 0.2 mile to the trail, then hike 0.3 mile to a short spur trail to Fall Creek Falls.

BIG FALL CREEK

There are several interesting scenes on the way to Chichester Falls. Turn off S.R. 58 at the Lowell exit, where an old covered bridge looks out of place above the reservoir of Lookout Point Lake. Follow the Lowell-Jasper Road through town and turn right (east) in 2.9 miles on Big Fall Creek Road just before reaching a second covered bridge. Take the secondary road, which becomes Road #181, for 15.9 miles to a turnout at Andy Creek.

Chichester Falls

This 20 to 30-foot punchbowl waterfall along Andy Creek is easiest and safest to view from the bridge. A casual observer may disagree with the rating, but a closer look reveals an interesting grotto around the plunge pool. Moss and plants enhance the setting.

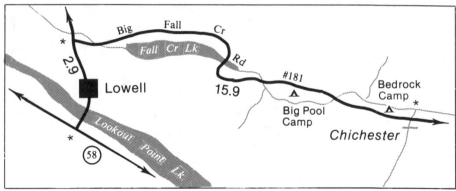

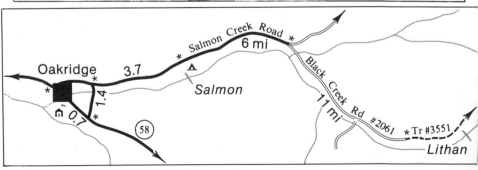

SALMON CREEK DRAINAGE

To reach these two waterfalls east of Oakridge, turn off S.R. 58 at Fish Hatchery Road. Follow the route 1.4 miles to its end, and turn right (east) on Salmon Creek Road.

Salmon Creek Falls

This small 5 to 10-foot drop is at the campground of the same name. Drive 3.7 miles along Salmon Creek Road to the camp.

Lithan Falls

Nettie Creek steeply cascades 50 to 100 feet. Follow Salmon Creek Road to the end of the pavement, then cross the creek at Black Creek Road #2061. Take Road #2061 to its end in an estimated 11 miles. Black Creek Trail #3551 starts here with the falls about two miles away. This descent is also known as *Lillian Falls*.

SALT CREEK DRAINAGE

There are four cataracts within two square miles in this area. Drive 21 miles east from Oakridge or six miles west from Willamette Pass along S.R. 58. Park at the designated turnout, or in Salt Creek Falls Campground.

Salt Creek Falls

This 286-foot plunge is near the road and can be viewed year-round. Trails and fenced vistas provide a variety of views of this impressive waterfall, which was discovered by Frank S. Warner and Charles Tufti in March, 1887.

Lower Falls Creek Falls

This double descent totals 30 to 50 feet. Begin hiking from the campground on Vivian Lake Trail #3662. Cross railroad tracks in one mile and follow an old dirt road for half a mile. Then hike up a steep trail leading half a mile to views of the falls.

Falls Creek Falls

This 40 to 60-foot plunge is visible from the ridge trail. Continue climbing steeply one mile past the lower falls. A sign tacked to a tree marks the viewpoint for the moderately distant falls.

Upper Falls Creek Falls

The best of the descents from Falls Creek is visible from the trail. Continue climbing about 0.2 mile along Trail #3662 past the main falls. The upper waterfall descends 50 to 80 feet.

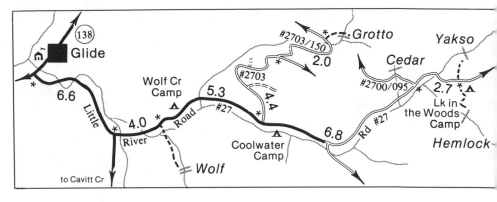

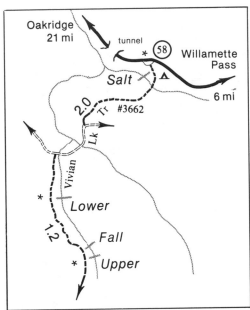

LITTLE RIVER DRAINAGE

Pass one descent after another as you progress up the Little River Valley. To reach it, turn off S.R. 138 at Glide onto Little River Road.

Wolf Creek Falls

Water slides down a mountainside in two parts. The upper portion drops 75 feet and the lower descent 50 feet. Drive 10.6 miles along Little River Road and stop at the parking area across the road from Wolf Creek Trailhead. The easily hiked trail leads to the falls on Bureau of Land Management land in two miles.

Cedar Creek Falls

Continue 12.1 miles past Wolf Creek along Little River Road #27. Turn left (north) on Road #2700/095 where a sign points toward Cedar Creek Falls. Drive one mile to a sharp switchback in the road. Water trickles 40 to 60 feet from the adjacent cliff. Wet your head if you dare!

Hemlock Falls

Drive along Little River Road #27 for 2.7 miles past Road #2700/095 to Lake in the Woods Camp. Hemlock Falls Trail #1520 begins just before you reach the campsites. Follow it down steeply half a mile to an 80-foot rush along Hemlock Creek.

Yakso Falls

Yakso Falls Trail #1519 starts across the road from the entrance to Lake in the Woods Camp. Walk 0.7 mile to the base of the 70-foot falls.

Grotto Falls

The shimmering waters of this pleasant waterfall plunge 100 feet along Emile Creek. Backtrack 9.5 miles from Lake in the Woods Camp. Or from Wolf Creek continue 5.3 miles east on Little River Road #27 to Road #2703. Drive 4.4 miles and turn left on Road #2703/150, following the gravel route two miles farther to Grotto Falls Trail #1503 on the far side of Emile Creek bridge. The trail goes behind the descent in 0.3 mile. This waterfall was once known as *Emile Falls,* after Emile Shivigny, who home-steaded nearby in 1875.

CAVITT CREEK

Cavitt Creek Falls

Take a foot bath in the refreshing pool at the base of this 10 to 15-foot descent. Turn right (south) off Little River Road onto Cavitt Creek Road 6.6 miles from Glide. In 3.3 miles, turn at the Bureau of Land Manage-ment-administered Cavitt Creek Falls Park. The waterfall is in the park.

Shadow Falls

This triple descent totaling 80 to 100 feet along Cavitt Creek is aptly named. Drive 8.1 miles past the park on Cavitt Creek Road #25. Stop at the turnout and follow Shadow Falls Trail #1504 to the descent in 0.8 mile.

The waterfall has worked its way headward over the past thousand years, eroding upstream through a rock fracture to form a narrow, natural grotto. Immediately downstream from the falls, next to the trail, are interesting weathered bedrock formations.

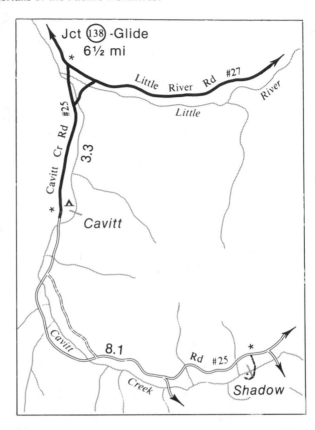

Jct (138) -Glide
6½ mi

Little River Rd #27

Little River

Cavitt Cr Rd #25

3.3

Cavitt

Cavitt

8.1

Rd #25

Creek

Shadow

Barr Creek Falls

Grotto Falls

IDLEYLD PARK AREA

Scenic S.R. 138 serves as a convenient corridor, passing many waterfalls on the way from Glide to Crater Lake.

Susan Creek Falls

A trail built by the Bureau of Land Management ascends one mile to this descent. Drive 7½ miles east from Idleyld Park to Susan Creek State Park. The trailhead is across the road from the park.

Fall Creek Falls

Drive four miles east from Susan Creek State Park to the marked turnout on S.R. 138. Fall Creek Falls National Recreation Trail winds around and through slabs of bedrock and past the natural, lush vegetation of Job's Garden. This beautiful path leads 0.9 mile to a double falls with each tier 35 to 50 feet in height.

STEAMBOAT

Fishing is prohibited in the entire drainage basin encompassing Steamboat Creek in order to provide undisturbed spawning grounds for the salmon and steelhead of the North Umpqua River drainage.

Little Falls

Watch the fish negotiate this 5 to 10-foot break along Steamboat Creek. Turn off S.R. 138 onto Steamboat Road #38 at Steamboat. Drive 1.1 miles to the undesignated turnout next to the falls and the adjacent bedrock slabs.

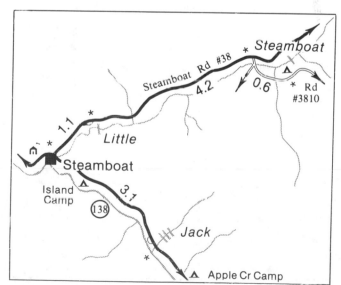

Steamboat Falls

Continue along Steamboat Road #38 for 4.2 miles past Little Falls. Turn right (east) on Road #3810 and continue to Steamboat Falls Campground entrance in 0.6 mile. A developed viewpoint showcases a 20 to 30-foot waterfall. Some fish attempt to jump the cataract, while others use the adjacent fish ladder.

Jack Falls

Park at the undesignated turnout at mile marker 42, located 3.1 miles east of Steamboat along S.R. 138. Walk 100 yards east to Jack Creek. Follow the brushy streambank to three closely grouped falls. The lower descent slides 20 to 30 feet in two segments. The middle and upper falls are of the horsetail type, descending 25 to 40 feet and 50 to 70 feet respectively.

TOKETEE

Toketee Falls

The Indian word Toketee means "graceful." It is an apt title for this inspiring waterfall. The major lower portion plunges 80 to 120 feet over a sheer wall of basalt, while the upper descent drops 25 to 40 feet. Turn off S.R. 138 toward Toketee Lake on Road #268. Drive 0.3 mile to the marked left (west) turn to the beginning of Toketee Falls Trail #1495. Follow the easily hiked path 0.6 mile to a viewpoint looking into the falls.

The Toketee Pipeline can be seen from the trailhead. Pacific Power diverts water from Toketee Lake via this 12-foot redwood stave pipe. It bypasses North Umpqua River for 1,663 feet to a mile long tunnel. The water then plunges down a steel penstock pipe to the Toketee Powerhouse where it can generate as much as 210,000 kilowatts of electricity.

Watson Falls

Drive 2.2 miles past Toketee Lake along S.R. 138 to Fish Creek Road #37. Follow it 0.2 mile to Watson Falls Picnic Ground. Follow Watson Falls Trail #1495 from the picnic area. A footbridge 0.3 mile from the trailhead provides a full view of Watson Creek hurtling down 272 feet.

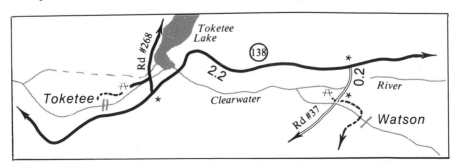

NORTHEASTERN UMPQUA

Whitehorse Falls

Relax on the porchlike vista overlooking this 10 to 15-foot punchbowl falls along Clearwater River. Turn off S.R. 138 at the marked turn for White-horse Falls Camp. Park at the picnic area adjacent to the falls.

Clearwater Falls

Drive 3½ miles east from Whitehorse Falls to the turnoff for Clearwater Falls Camp. Follow the access road 0.2 mile to the picnic area. The 30-foot cascade is a short walk up Clearwater River.

Lemolo Falls

The previous settings are conducive to meditation, but this 75 to 100-foot monster along the North Umpqua River is more stirring. Turn north from S.R. 138 three miles east of Clearwater Falls and drive toward Lemolo Lake. Bear left (north) after 4.6 miles to Thorn Prairie Road #3401, then turn right at Lemolo Falls Road #3401/800. The trailhead is 2.2 miles farther. Lemolo Falls Trail #1468 descends steeply one mile to the base of the falls. Lemolo is Chinook for "wild" or "untamed."

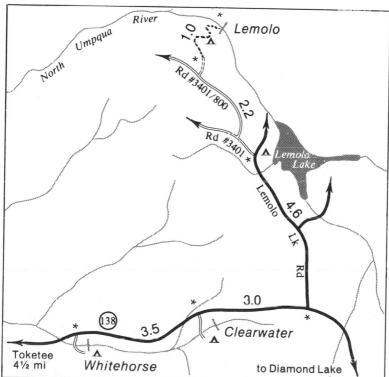

FALLS OF THE UPPER ROGUE

Upper Falls

Upper Rogue River Trail passes next to two falls along its northerly route. The closest trailheads are at Mazama Viewpoint, 0.6 mile west of S.R. 138 on S.R. 230, and Hamaker Campground, 11 miles north of S.R. 62 off S.R. 230. The steep 30 to 50-foot cascades of the upper cataract is 3½ miles south of Mazama Viewpoint. The 15 to 25-foot drop of *Middle Falls* is 1½ miles downstream from the upper falls, or 2½ miles upstream from Hamaker Camp.

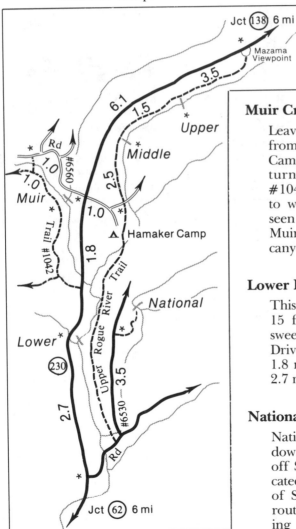

Muir Creek Falls

Leave S.R. 230 at Road #6560 across from the access road to Hamaker Camp. Drive about one mile to a turnout for Buck Canyon Trail #1042. Hike one mile downstream to where Sherwood Creek can be seen falling 15 to 25 feet in tiers into Muir Creek on the other side of the canyon.

Lower Falls

This block-type waterfall drops 10 to 15 feet where S.R. 230 follows a sweeping bend in the Rogue River. Drive to an undesignated turnout 1.8 miles south of Road #6560, or 2.7 miles north of Road #6530

National Creek Falls

National creek pours 30 to 50 feet downward in three segments. Turn off S.R. 230 onto Road #6530, located 5.8 miles north of the junction of S.R. 62. Follow this secondary route 3½ miles to the marked parking area for National Creek Falls Trail #1053. The path descends moderately to the base of the falls in half a mile.

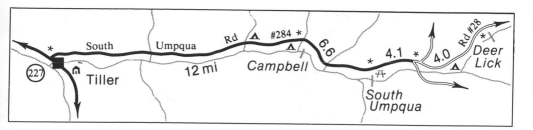

SOUTH UMPQUA

Campbell Falls

Drive to the hamlet of Tiller along S.R. 227. Turn northeast onto South Umpqua Road #284 northwest of the ranger station and continue 12 miles to Boulder Creek Camp. The waterfall is on the Umpqua above the mouth of Boulder Creek. The name honors Robert G. Campbell, a former U.S. Forest Service employee who was killed in action during World War II.

South Umpqua Falls

Water slides 10 to 15 feet over wide slabs of bedrock. Drive 6.6 miles past Boulder Creek Camp to South Umpqua Falls Picnic Area and Observation Point. A fish ladder bypasses the falls.

Deer Lick Falls

Peer into a series of five blocklike descents ranging from 5 to 20 feet in height. Reach them by driving 4.1 miles past the previous entry along South Umpqua Road #284. Do not cross the river, but bear left on Road #28 toward Camp Comfort. The waterfall is along Black Rock Fork four miles beyond the campground on Road #28.

AZALEA AREA

Cow Creek Falls

Cow Creek drops 25 to 40 feet along a series of rock steps. Turn off Interstate 5 at Azalea (Exit 88) and follow Cow Creek Road for 17.2 miles to Devils Flat Camp. A short loop trail across the road from the campground passes the falls. Two historic buildings from homestead days are landmarks near the trail.

MILL CREEK SCENIC AREA

Three of the following five waterfalls are part of Boise Cascade Corporation's Mill Creek Falls Scenic Area. The timber company has constructed public trails on some of its unspoiled land.

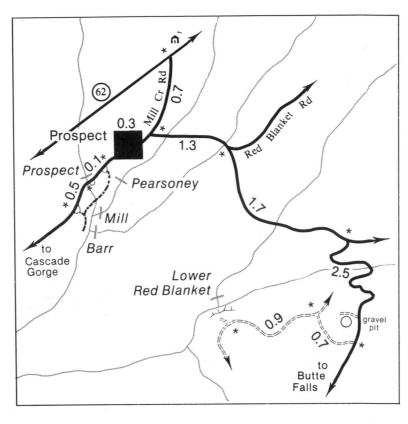

Mill Creek Falls

Look across a canyon cut by the Rogue River to this thundering 173-foot plunge. Turn off S.R. 62 onto Mill Creek Road at either Cascade Gorge or Prospect. Park at the turnout marked by a large trail system sign. Start on the interpretive trail immediately south of the parking area and walk 0.3 mile to the viewpoint.

Barr Creek Falls

Follow the trail 0.1 mile past Mill Creek Falls to a rocky outcrop for a superb view across the canyon to this 175 to 200-foot display. The cataract is also known as *Bear Creek Falls*.

Prospect Falls

Drive half a mile past the Mill Creek parking area to an undesignated turnout on the east side of the bridge. A well-trod path leads to many good views of Rogue River tumbling 50 to 100 feet. I've called the waterfall by the name of the nearby town.

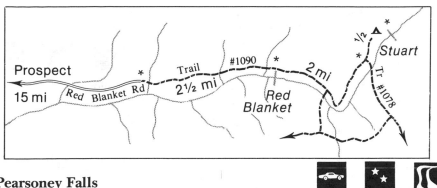

Pearsoney Falls

Continue 0.1 mile north of the bridge over the Rogue to a parking area off Mill Creek Road. Follow the main trail 0.2 mile to where Mill Creek drops 15 to 25 feet. The waterfall is named after two early pioneer families of the Prospect Area: the Pearsons and the Mooneys.

Lower Red Blanket Falls

Take Red Blanket Road from Prospect and turn right after 1.3 miles. Continue 1.7 miles, then bear right (south) toward Butte Falls. After the route switchbacks uphill, look for a jeep trail to the right (west). It's the first road past a short gravel road ending at a gravel pit.

Follow the dirt road for 1.6 miles as shown on the accompanying map. Park at the short, abandoned jeep trail which leads toward the canyon rim. Follow the trail for a few hundred yards, then cut through the woods toward the roaring sound of the falls. Pick a route partway down the moderately steep slope for good views of Red Blanket Creek plummeting 90 to 140 feet into the opposite side of the Rogue River. The walk is about 0.3 mile, but I recommend it for experienced hikers only.

SKY LAKES WILDERNESS

Red Blanket Falls

Follow Red Blanket Road for 15 miles from Prospect to the parking area for Upper Red Blanket Trail #1090. Red Blanket Creek drops 20 feet about 2½ miles upstream from the trailhead.

Stuart Falls

Continue two miles past the previous descent to the end of Trail #1090. Follow Stuart Falls Trail #1078 to the left (north) for half a mile to where Red Blanket Creek veils down 25 feet. A campsite is nearby.

CRATER LAKE NATIONAL PARK

The center of attraction in the park is the *caldera,* an enormous depression presently occupied by Crater Lake. It formed as a result of a cataclysmic eruption of volcanic Mount Mazama 6,600 years ago. Heavy annual precipitation maintains the lake level. In addition to the lake, the park has a pair of falls.

Annie Falls

For a canyon rim view of water rushing 30 to 50 feet along Annie Creek, drive 4.7 miles north of the south park entrance to a turnout off S.R. 62. Heed the warning signs at the canyon rim. The slopes are very unstable and impossible to walk on.

Vidae Falls

Vidae Creek sprays from Crater Lake's south rim near Applegate Peak. Drive three miles southeast from the park headquarters to a turnout near the falls.

BUTTE FALLS

Butte Falls

The nearby community is named for this 10 to 15-foot block waterfall. Turn off S.R. 62 at the Butte Falls junction five miles north of Eagle Point. Reach the town of Butte Falls in 16 miles. Upon entering the village, look for Pine Street to the left (north). Backtrack one block to an unmarked gravel road. Take this unpaved route, past a waste treatment plant to an undesignated parking area in 0.6 mile. Well-worn paths lead shortly to the falls.

Vidae Falls

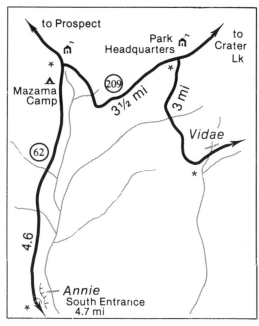

THE COLUMBIA PLATEAU

The landscape of eastern Oregon is dominated by a broad region of generally low relief called the Columbia Plateau. This plain, which extends into southeastern Washington, northern Nevada, and southwestern Idaho, is composed of thick layers of basalt which formed from widespread lava flows 30 million years ago. Waterfalls are scarce in the Oregon portion of the plateau for two reasons. First, major rivers lack descents because of the consistant erosion resistance of the basaltic bedrock. Second, low annual precipitation means that few tributary streams flow over the rims of the larger river canyons.

Most of the cataracts in this region are found where additional geomorphic processes have led to waterfall formation in local areas. Recent lava flows inundated the course of the Deschutes River 5,000 to 6,000 years ago. When the lava cooled, jumbled basaltic rock was formed. The river cuts into and tumbles over these rocky obstructions.

The Strawberry Mountains near the town of John Day were shaped by the accumulation of basalt, rhyolite, and breccia due to volcanic activities 10 to 13 million years ago. The extreme differences in the erosion resistance of these rock types produces waterfalls where streams flow across their contact points.

The Wallowa Mountains of northeastern Oregon are in one of the few nonvolcanic areas of the region. Large masses of granite and sedimentary rocks were displaced thousands of feet above the surrounding plain 100 to 150 million years ago. Its high relief stopped subsequent lava at its western perimeter. Since the Wallowas rise over 8,000 feet above sea level, their climate was sufficiently cold and moist for alpine glaciation to occur 10,000 years ago. The erosive work of these glaciers left vertical breaks for stream courses to plunge over.

REDMOND

The Deschutes River (meaning River of the Falls) is aptly titled, since it has nine cataracts along its course from La Pine to Culver. Five are near Redmond. Unfortunately *Cline Falls* is the only accessible one. The unapproachable descents are *Awbrey Falls*, named after Marshall Clay Awbrey, who served in the Rogue River Indian War of the mid-1800s; *Big Falls; Odin Falls*, titled after the mythological Norse god of wisdom and heroes; and *Steelhead Falls*, presumably named for the fish.

Cline Falls

The force of this cascade is reduced because a portion of the river has been diverted to a rustic powerhouse nearby. Drive 4½ miles west of Redmond on S.R. 126. Turn right (north) at the west side of the river on Southwest Eagle Drive. Park at the entrance to a dirt road 0.3 mile farther and look into the canyon at the falls and power facility. The descent was named for Dr. C.A. Cline, who once owned the falls.

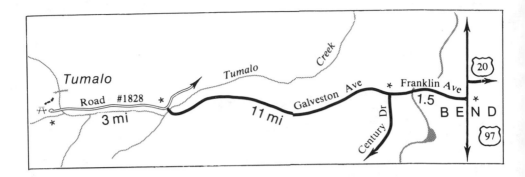

TUMALO CREEK

Tumalo Falls

Turn off U.S. 97 in Bend onto westbound Franklin Avenue. The street becomes Galveston Avenue in one mile at Drake City Park. Proceed west 11 miles and turn on graveled Road #1828. Continue three miles to Tumalo Falls Picnic Area. In 1982 when I visited the falls, this access road was closed to public vehicles, so I hiked the final three miles along the road.

This 97-foot plummet is framed by stark tree snags—brown remnants of a forest fire during the summer of 1979. Think of your favorite vacation spots and imagine them devastated by fire. The Tumalo scene is a graphic reminder that "only you can prevent forest fires."

LAVA BUTTE GEOLOGICAL AREA

The Deschutes River drops in three places on the western fringe of Lava Butte Geological Area. Drive toward Tumalo Falls (see TUMALO CREEK), but turn on Cascade Lakes Highway (also known as Century Drive) from the west side of Bend. Continue 6.3 miles and turn left (south) on gravelled Road #1808 at the sign to Dillon Falls.

Lava Island Falls

The waterfall is minor, but the jumbled lava rock being split by the Deschutes is intriguing. Follow Road #1808 south for 0.4 mile from Century Drive. Turn left (east) on dirt Road #1831 and continue to its north end in 0.8 mile.

Dillon Falls

Take Road #1808 three miles south from Century Drive. Turn left (southeast) on dirt Road #1818 and drive to its end in 0.9 mile. A trail goes from the parking area to views of a quarter mile long chasm where water froths 40 to 60 feet. There are no fenced observation points from the rim. The descent is named for homesteader Leander Dillon.

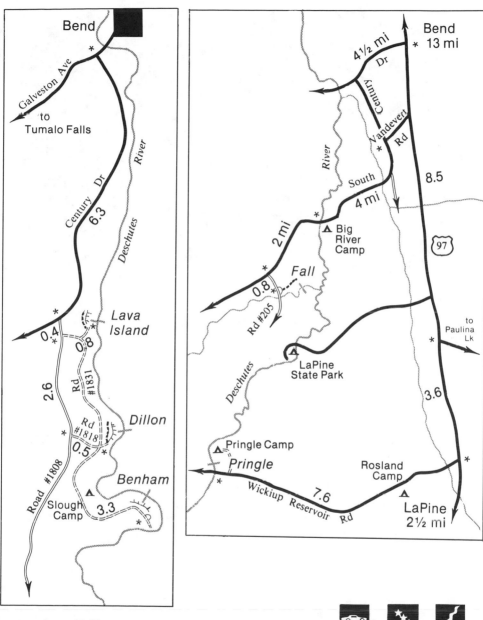

Benham Falls

Bear south on Road #1831 at its four-way intersection with Road #1818. Park where the road meets the river in 3.3 miles. The descent is immediately downstream. A short pathway leads to secure, but unfenced views of the river shooting down 40 to 60 feet through a narrow canyon. The waterfall is named for J.R. Benham, who unsuccessfully filed for land nearby in 1885.

Fall River Falls

LA PINE AREA

Fall River Falls

Leave U.S. 97 at South Century Drive 13 miles south of Bend. Drive 10½ miles and turn left (south) on dirt Road #205. Park at the wide turnout preceding Fall River bridge. Follow the jeep trail 0.2 mile from the parking area to grassy banks surrounded by pines. The river tumbles 10 to 15 feet.

Pringle Falls

Although pictured in travel guides and labeled on road maps, the main part of this series of small falls and cascades can no longer be seen by the public. A housing development currently lines the Deschutes along the descent. From the security system, it is clear that visitors are not welcome. Only uninspiring views of the beginning and end of the falls remain.

Turn toward Wickiup Reservoir 2½ miles north of La Pine at the junction of U.S. 97 and the access road. Drive 7.6 miles to the bridge crossing at the headwaters of the falls. Pringle Falls Camp is immediately downstream from the end of the falls. Follow dirt Road #218 to the campground. The descent is named for O.M. Pringle, who bought land nearby in 1902.

NEWBERRY CRATER

A dominant feature of the geology south of Bend is a *shield volcano*. It postdates and contrasts with the great *composite volcanos* of the Cascade Range (Mount Rainier, Mount Hood, Mount Shasta, and others). Shield volcanoes are typically larger, but have gentler slopes than the composite type. The Paulina

Mountains are part of a shield volcano. Their Newberry Crater represents a *caldera,* where the central portion fo the volcano collapsed. Paulina Lake and East Lake currently fill the depression. As Paulina Creek flows from Paulina Lake, its erosive power has cut through the volcano's layers of basalt at a greater rate than through more resistant rhyolite. Waterfalls occur where these two rock layers meet along the stream's course.

Lower Falls

Paulina Creek descends a total of 50 to 80 feet as the creek diverges along its upper portion before fanning out below. Turn off U.S. 97 toward Paulina Lake six miles north of La Pine. Drive ten miles to a large, undesignated parking area to the left (north). Hike along an old jeep trail beginning at the far end of the turnout. At a junction in 0.4 mile, bear left (west) and walk 0.6 mile until the falls can be heard. An unmarked trail from the jeep route leads across a footbridge over the creek and downstream to views of the falls. The rating decreases during the low water periods of late summer.

Paulina Creek Falls

This 100-foot segmented waterfall is best seen in early summer when the stream flows heaviest. Continue 2.9 miles past Lower Falls along the paved road. Stop at Paulina Creek Falls Picnic Ground. A short trail leads to a developed vista with superb views. The waterfall is also known as *Upper Falls.*

Paulina Falls

STRAWBERRY MOUNTAINS WILDERNESS

The Strawberry Mountains rise 3,500 to 5,000 feet above the surrounding Columbia Plateau. Their climate, cooler and moister than the lower plateau, is suitable for forests.

Drive to Prairie City on U.S. 26 and obtain a backpacking permit at the local ranger station. The wilderness trails are generally clear of snow from mid-June to mid-November. Leave the main highway at Prairie City, following the Strawberry Lake signs south from town. Gravelled Strawberry Road #1428 ends and the trail begins at Strawberry Camp in 12½ miles.

Strawberry Falls

Start hiking on Strawberry Basin Trail #375 from the south end of the campground. Reach Strawberry Lake in 1½ miles and the base of the falls in a total of 3½ miles. The trail continues to the top of the cataract in 0.2 mile. Strawberry Creek reportedly drops 75 feet.

Slide Falls

Hike one mile along Strawberry Basin Trail #375, then bear left (east) at Slide Basin Trail #372. This pathway steepens until it reaches the ridgetop in one mile, then follows along Slide Creek Valley. After three miles, a sign points east toward the descent along Slide Creek.

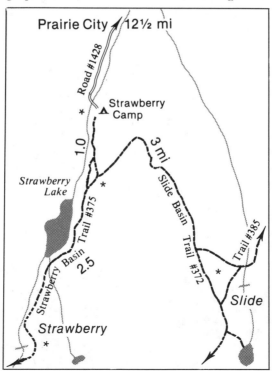

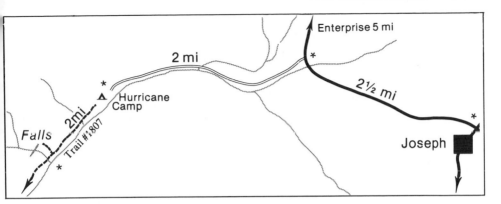

HURRICANE CREEK DRAINAGE

Falls Creek Falls

To reach this waterfall near the northeastern flank of the High Wallawas, drive along S.R. 82 to the western-style community of Joseph. At the north end of town, turn right (west) at the marked turnoff to Imnaha. Be sure to turn **away** from Imnaha at the junction, not toward it. In 2½ miles, bear left at Hurricane Creek. The gravel road ends at a campsite in two miles. Hike two miles from the campground along Hurricane Creek Trail #1807 to the first trail junction to the right (west). This spur path leads up Falls Creek to its descent in a quarter mile.

WALLOWA LAKE AREA

Wallowa Lake is a beautiful example of a *paternoster lake,* a body of water formed by a natural dam blocking part of a glacial valley. Drive through Joseph on S.R. 82 to Wallowa Lake State Park in six miles. Turn left (south) toward the picnic area and away from the main boating and camping facilities.

Wallowa Falls

West Fork Trail #1820 toward Ice Lake starts at the picnic area. A footbridge crosses East Fork Wallowa River, then ascends shortly to a rocky outcrop adjacent to the West Fork in 0.1 mile. From this natural vista, follow the ridge a short distance downstream to a well-worn path above the river. From the trail you can see West Fork Wallowa River pouring down 30 to 50 feet.

Adam Creek Falls

The hiker views this series of descents individually, while the tourist sees them collectively. Hike three miles along West Fork Trail #1820, then turn right (west) on Ice Lake Trail #18 and continue two miles to Adam Creek. You will pass several waterfalls during the next two miles.

Tourists atop Mount Howard can view the tiered falls as silvery mountainside threads. Take the High Wallowas gondola 3,700 feet above the valley for unforgettable views of Eagle Cap Wilderness, Wallowa Lake, and the Columbia Plateau. Look for the falls to the southwest.

ADEL

Deep Creek Falls

This 30 to 50-foot cataract is framed by columns of basalt in a sagebrush setting. It is next to S.R. 140 at the floor of narrow and steep Deep Creek Canyon. Drive about 2¾ miles west from Adel or 35 miles east from Lakeview for roadside views.

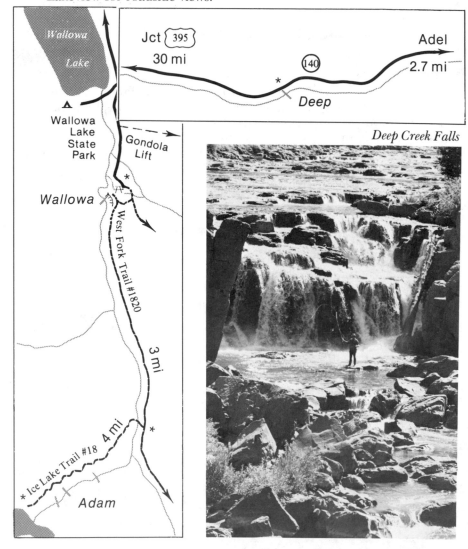

Deep Creek Falls

THE IDAHO PANHANDLE

The Panhandle of Northern Idaho separates Washington from Montana. From the Canadian border 170 miles south to Lewiston, its width varies from 45 to 125 miles. Although many states have unusual shapes, Idaho's is unique in its historical and political significance. No other state was shaped wholly by the divisions of its neighbors. Idaho is the land not annexed by Montana, Wyoming, Utah, Nevada, Oregon, or Washington.

The Panhandle is a region of large lakes and rolling to rugged mountains. *Coeur D'Alene Lake*, *Lake Pend Oreille*, *Priest Lake*, and *Dworshak Reservoir* cover large areas. All but Dworshak are natural. Mountain ranges such as the Selkirks, the Purcells, the Bitterroots, and the Clearwaters are distributed through the region. The Panhandle has 31 recognized waterfalls, of which 25 are described here.

Geomorphologists, scientists who study landforms, classify waterfalls as *destructive* or *constructive*. Most cataracts, including all the known ones of the Pacific Northwest, are of the destructive variety. The force of running water slowly erodes their stream beds, sometimes causing the falls to recede upstream. Constructive descents, on the other hand, mostly flow from mineral deposits and migrate downstream as the deposits accumulate. The trickling descents from Mammoth Hot Springs in Yellowstone National Park are constructive falls.

Destructive falls are further classified by how they developed. *Consequent falls* are located where a preexisting break occurs along the course of a stream. An example is water plunging into a glacier-carved valley, as at *Copper Falls*. When streams erode along rock materials of varying rates of resistance, *subsequent falls* may form, as at *Snow Creek Falls*.

The waterfalls of the Northwest can be enjoyed for their beauty alone, but they are even more interesting when the forces that created them are considered.

PRIEST RIVER DRAINAGE

Torrelle Falls

A rustic restaurant built over the stream at the base of this 10 to 15-foot waterfall makes it unique. Drive 8½ miles north from the town of Priest River on S.R. 57. The waterfall is on the left (west) side of the highway along West Branch Priest River.

Mission Falls

Continue north on S.R. 57 for 11½ miles past the previous falls. Park at the northeast side of the bridge crossing Upper West Branch Priest River.

Follow a jeep trail next to the bridge for 0.2 mile to a road junction. Take the right fork; the left quickly leads back to the paved road. Follow the dirt route for 1.7 miles, bearing right at all junctions. When you near the river, a well-worn trail leads to the falls in a few hundred yards.

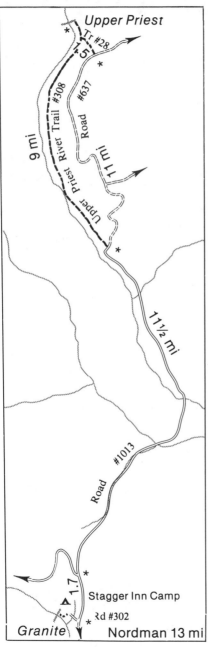

PRIEST LAKE

Recreational activities continue year-round near the 26,000 acres of Priest Lake, but the area's waterfalls are remote and should be visited from early summer to late autumn.

Granite Falls

Drive 37 miles north of Priest River along S.R. 57 to Nordman. Continue 13 miles to the entrance road to Stagger Inn Camp and Granite Falls. S.R. 57 becomes Granite Creek Road #302 two miles past Nordman. The trailhead sign to the falls may be misleading. Do not cross the log over the stream to which the arrow points. Instead walk straight past the sign. Granite Creek slides 50 to 75 feet less than 100 yards away. This descent is actually in Washington, but I've listed it in the Panhandle section because the primary access is from Idaho.

Upper Priest Falls

Upper Priest River in the secluded northwest tip of Idaho noisily crashes 100 to 125 feet. Drive 1¾ miles past Stagger Inn Camp, turning right (northeast) on Road #308. The path follows the river for nine miles and ends at the falls.

There is another route to the falls, according to the 1981 version of the National Forest Travel Plan. Follow primitive Road #637 for about 11 miles to Continental Trail #28. This trail meets with Trail #308 about 1½ miles from the falls. The descent is also known as *American Falls* to distinguish it from the similar *Canadian Falls,* located upstream in British Columbia.

PEND OREILLE

A few years ago, the easiest route to Char Falls and Wellington Creek Falls was on Lightning Creek Road from Clark Fork. But severe flooding in 1980 all but destroyed the middle and lower parts of the road. Fortunately, an alternate route is available. The trip is rougher, but worthwhile. However, you must wait until the snow melts in midsummer.

Rapid Lightning Falls

Water rushes 20 to 30 feet along Rapid Lightning Creek. Turn off U.S. 2/95 onto S.R. 200 and drive 6.2 miles before turning again on Colburn-Culver Road. In 2.9 miles, turn right (east) at the schoolhouse onto the road marked Rapid Lightning Creek. Park at an undesignated turnout 3.4 miles farther. The cataract is accessible from short, well-trod paths.

Char Falls

   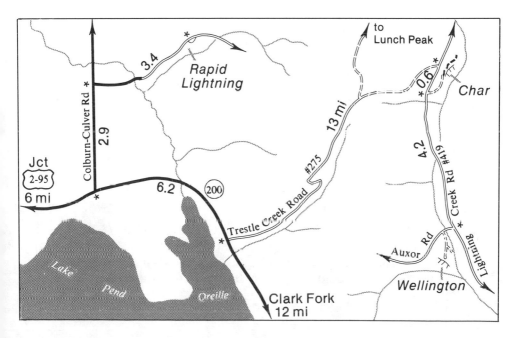

Drive along S.R. 200 another 6.2 miles east past Colburn-Culver Road to Trestle Creek Road #275. Follow this road for 13 miles to Lightning Creek Road #419. Turn right (south) and continue 0.6 mile to a primitive road to the left. Park and follow the rocky road half a mile to a wide trail at its end. Take the trail only twenty yards, then find a faint path to the right. It leads to an overlook of the falls in less than 100 yards. Lightning Creek descends powerfully for 50 to 75 feet.

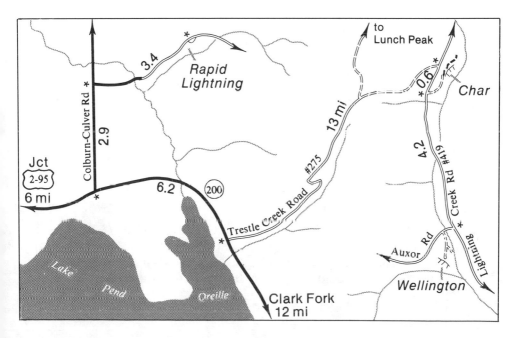

Wellington Creek Falls

Continue 4.2 miles past Char Falls along Lightning Creek Road #419 to Auxor Road. Cross Lightning Creek and drive or hike down the primitive road to the left. Bear right at the fork in 0.4 mile and continue 0.4 mile on the bumpy road to its end. Walk toward the creek and a bit upstream, listening for the falls. Continue toward Wellington Creek for good over-views of the wonderful 50 to 75-foot waterfall and the lush vegetation surrounding it. Be careful near the edge of the precipice.

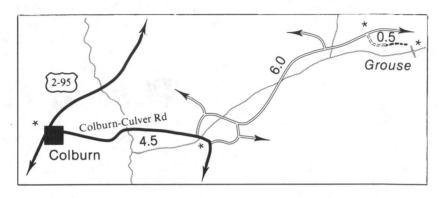

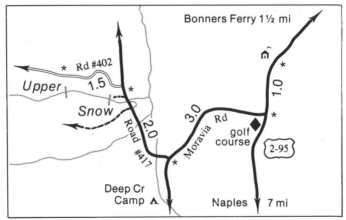

COLBURN AREA

Grouse Falls

Grouse Creek cuts through bedrock in a small series of descents totaling 15 to 20 feet. Turn off U.S. 2/95 at Colburn onto Colburn-Culver Road. Drive east 4½ miles and turn left on the gravel road. Continue six miles up Grouse Creek Valley to a turnout near a dirt road to the right. Park and follow the road which becomes a trail in 0.3 mile. The descent is 0.2 mile farther.

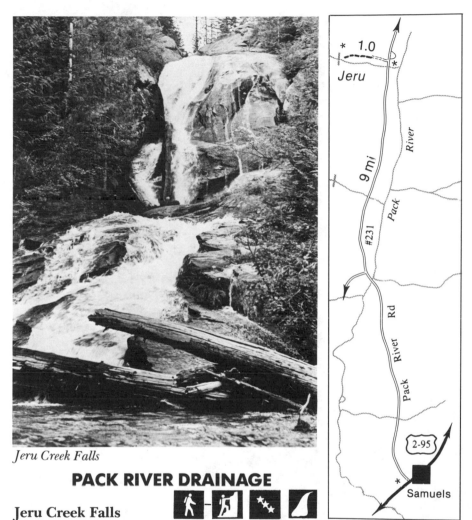

Jeru Creek Falls

PACK RIVER DRAINAGE

Jeru Creek Falls

Turn off U.S. 2/95 at Samuels onto Pack River Road #231. Drive nine miles to the undesignated turnout on the north side of Jeru Creek. The one-mile trek from the road starts on an obsolete four-wheel-drive route and eventually turns into a seldom used, unmaintained trail. When the path seems to end, you should be near the 100 to 150-foot waterfall. There is a similar descent along nearby Hellroaring Creek, but unfortunately, it is not accessible.

BONNERS FERRY

Snow Creek Falls

Drive 2½ miles south of Bonners Ferry on U.S. 2/95. Turn onto Moravia Road at the golf course. Bear right in three miles on West Side Road #417

and drive two miles to a turnout and informal campsite. The unnamed trail on the north side of Snow Creek leads shortly to the base of the segmented 50 to 75-foot falls. The named trail south of the creek goes up the ridge and does not provide any views of the descent.

The 75 to 125-foot drop of the *Upper Falls* is more impressive than its lower counterpart, but there is no direct access. You can catch a bird's eye glimpse of the falls from Snow Creek Road #402 about 1½ miles from where it intersects West Side Road #417.

MOYIE RIVER

Moyie Falls is purported to be one of Idaho's great scenic attractions. No argument here. But contrary to what some sources imply, you can't get good views from the main highway. The following description, however, directs you to a picture perfect vista.

Moyie Falls

Turn off U.S. 2 at the Moyie Springs exit immediately west of the Moyie River bridge. After half a mile, turn left on the street adjacent to a lumber yard. Follow this residential road half a mile to various turnouts offering good views into a canyon carved out over thousands of years. Moyie River absolutely thunders through in a tiered cataract. The larger upper portion crashes 60 to 100 feet beneath an antiquated span crossing the canyon. The lower portion cascades 20 to 40 feet.

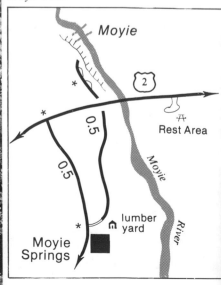

Moyie Falls

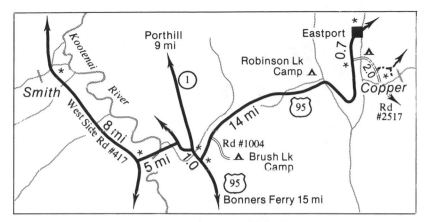

BOUNDARY LINE

Smith Falls

Turn onto S.R. 1 from U.S. 95 at the junction about 15 miles north of Bonners Ferry. Drive one mile, then turn left (west) and continue five miles on the paved surface, crossing Kootenai River at the halfway point. Turn right (north) on West Side Road #417 and drive eight miles to a marked turnout to the falls. A heavy volume of water plunges 60 feet along Smith Creek. The descent and the viewpoint are on private property. Please obey the posted restrictions so others can continue to enjoy this setting.

Copper Falls

Turn off U.S. 95 onto Road #2517 less than three-fourths mile south of Eastport border crossing or 14 miles northeast of the junction of S.R. 1. Follow this bumpy gravel road for two miles to Copper Falls Trail #207. Hike a quarter mile along the moderately steep trail to the falls. Copper Creek hurtles down 160 feet.

MULLAN

Pass the historic mining towns of Kellogg, Wallace, and Mullan as you travel east from Coeur D'Alene along Interstate 90. (They may become *exclusively* historic if the depressed mining industry continues its slide through the 1980s.) Several nice waterfalls accessible from late summer to early autumn are located near the Bitterroot Divide which separates Idaho from Montana.

Willow Creek Falls

Leave Interstate 90 at Mullan (Exit 68). Drive through the town and continue east. The route turns right after 1½ miles and becomes Willow Creek Road. Continue 1½ miles, passing I-90, to the road's end near an

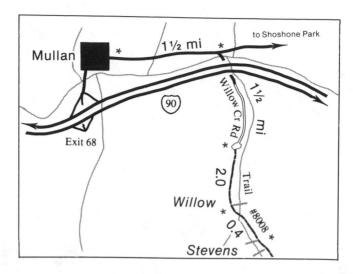

old set of railroad tracks. Willow Creek Trail #8008 leads moderately upstream for two miles to the 10 to 20-foot cascade along East Fork Willow Creek.

Stevens Lake Falls

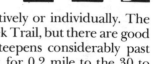

The tiers of this descent can be viewed collectively or individually. The cataracts are not easily visible from Willow Creek Trail, but there are good vantage points just off the path. The trail steepens considerably past Willow Creek Falls as it follows the East Fork for 0.2 mile to the 30 to 50-foot plunge of the lower portion. Hike 0.2 mile farther for a close-up view of the horsetail form of the 30 to 50-foot upper drop. Both portions can be glimpsed along the trail before they are reached.

ST. JOE DRAINAGE

The St. Joe River is particularly known for two things: First, it is navigable to one of the highest elevations of any river in North America. Second, its sport fishing is regarded as excellent, especially along the remote upper reaches where you can practically jump across the "mighty" St. Joe.

Falls Creek Falls

If you're heading upstream to catch some trout, pause at this 20 to 30-foot waterfall. Turn off S.R. 3 onto the St. Joe River Road half a mile northeast of St. Maries. The falls is 15 miles up the River Road, or 4½ miles past Shadowy St. Joe Camp. Park at the turnout nearest Falls Creek bridge.

ELK CREEK FALLS RECREATION AREA

The name may imply that the area is developed, but this is not the case. The term "recreation area" is a designation intended only to preserve the scenic

Lower Elk Falls

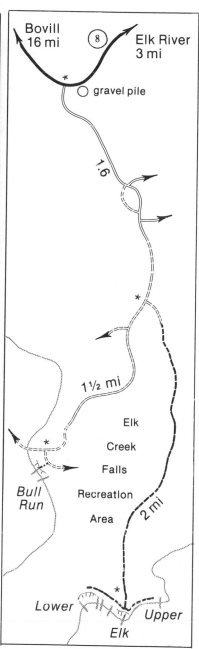

surroundings. Routes in the area are tolerable, but not clearly posted. Drive from Bovill toward Elk River on S.R. 8. After 16 miles, turn right (south) on an unmarked road next to a large gravel pile. Continue 1.6 miles and park at a major fork in the road.

Upper Elk Falls

Hike along the left fork of the road, which soon becomes a moderately sloped trail. Walk for two miles to a small open area, then descend quickly to the grassy slopes of the north rim of the canyon. Turn left, following a trail back into the woods and toward the creek. The 30 to 50-foot drop is about 0.3 mile upstream.

Elk Falls

This 125 to 150-foot cataract is the highest of the six along Elk Creek. At the canyon rim, follow the trail to the right among grassy slopes. There are many views of the falls during the next quarter mile.

Middle Elk Falls

This 20 to 30-foot descent a quarter mile downstream from the main falls can be looked down on from near the trail.

Twin Falls and Small Falls

These two waterfalls can be seen together from the trail. One is a 10 to 20-foot segmented descent; the other drops 10 to 20 feet in a punchbowl form. They are 0.1 mile past Middle Elk Falls.

Lower Elk Falls

Walk to the end of the well-worn trail about 0.1 mile past Small Falls. Carefully follow the faint path to the top of the rocky basaltic outcrop for an excellent view. This 75 to 100-foot plunge is the most powerful of the Elk Creek Falls. I recommend it only for cautious hikers who are not deterred by unfenced heights.

Bull Run Creek Falls

Instead of parking at the trailhead for Elk Creek Canyon, continue along the roadway, taking the forks as shown on the accompanying map. Park in 1½ miles. A small, faint path leads shortly to these 75 to 100-foot cascades.

Lower Falls

Return to the road from Bull Run Creek Falls and continue downstream along the ridge for 0.1 mile. After passing a small marshy area, scramble down the steep, timbered slope to the creek below the base of the 30 to 50-foot falls. I recommend this waterfall for determined bushwackers only.

WILDERNESS AREAS OF CENTRAL IDAHO

The interior of Idaho is dominated by swift rivers cutting deep canyons through rugged mountains. This sparsely populated region contains the largest tracts of wilderness in the continental United States. Three million acres of primitive expanse are set aside for the adventurer: The Selway-Bitterroot, Gospel Hump, and Sawtooth Wilderness Areas; the Hells Canyon and Sawtooth National Recreation Areas; and Salmon Wild and Scenic River.

The geology of this region is largely determined by the history of the *Idaho Batholith.* During the late Mesozoic era, 75 to 100 million years ago, extensive intrusions of magma crystallized in the subsurface of central Idaho. Rocks ranging from igneous granite and diorite to metamorphic gneisses were formed. Over the next 50 million years, the batholith was uplifted into mountains.

The mountainous terrain of the Idaho interior has been shaped mostly by erosion. Alpine glaciers carved the batholith at least four times over the last two million years, sharpening peaks and widening valleys. Most waterfalls of the region were created by glaciation. *Warbonnet Falls* descends from a mountainside into a glacial valley. Other streams follow along valleys and encounter obstacles called *moraines*—linear rock depositions left by glacial activity. *Lady Face Falls,* for instance, breaks through and drops over a moraine.

Stream erosion also contributes to the configuration of the batholith. The Salmon, Snake, Selway, and Lochsa Rivers have carved impressive canyons and gorges. Waterfalls tumble into these powerful waterways from tributaries which erode at a slower rate than the main rivers. *Fountain Creek Falls* and *Tumble Creek Falls* are examples. Cascades such as *Selway Falls* and *Carey Falls* are encountered where heterogenous rock material is eroded unevenly by rivers.

Because of the wild nature of central Idaho, large descents remain to be found, described, and mapped. Many of these cataracts are accessible only by plane, but a good share await discovery by hikers and backpackers. This book describes 33 of the 66 falls recognized within the central interior.

SELWAY RIVER

The Selway River begins in the interior of the Selway-Bitterroot Wilderness. As it flows from the wilderness area, its waters become a river of substantial magnitude. Farther downstream at Lowell the Selway meets the Lochsa River to become Middle Fork Clearwater River.

Selway Falls

Turn off U.S. 12 at Lowell and drive 18 miles to the end of Selway River Road. The river cascades 50 feet down beside the gravel roadway.

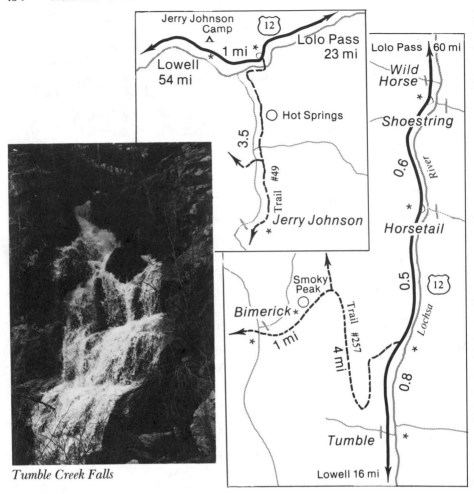

Tumble Creek Falls

LOCHSA DRAINAGE

U.S. 12 faithfully parallels the Lochsa River from its beginning near Lolo Pass to its confluence with the Selway 78 miles downstream. There are plenty of campsites along this stretch of the highway, but no vehicle service is available from Lolo Hot Springs to Lowell. Be sure your automobile has a full tank of gas before you start. Several waterfalls pour from tributary streams into the Lochsa within a two-mile stretch 16 to 18 miles northeast of Lowell near U.S. 12.

Tumble Creek Falls

Tumble Creek veils 20 to 30 feet before flowing beneath the main highway into the Lochsa River. Look for this descent along the east side of U.S. 12 between mile markers 113 and 114. I've called this waterfall by the name of its creek.

Bimerick Falls

Park 0.8 mile north of Tumble Creek at the turnout for the start of Trail #257. The trail steeply ascends to Smoky Peak in four miles. Drop down to the drainage basin in one additional mile. The cataract is next to the trail. I recommend this trip for experienced hikers only since my source indicated that the trail is not maintained annually by the Forest Service.

Horsetail Falls

At a sign by the road, look across the Lochsa to where Horsetail Falls descends 60 to 100 feet from an unnamed stream. Drive to a marked turnoff from the main highway between mile markers 114 and 115.

Shoestring Falls

View this descent from across the river at the marked turnout between mile markers 115 and 116. Water stairsteps 150 to 200 feet in five sections where an unnamed creek drops into Lochsa River.

Wild Horse Creek Falls

Park at the Shoestring Falls turnout and walk 0.1 mile along U.S. 12 to this double cataract from which water slides a total of 40 to 60 feet. I've called the descent by the name of the stream.

WARM SPRINGS CREEK

Warm Springs Creek derives its name from thermal waters flowing into the stream from Jerry Johnson Hot Springs. Most hikers head for the rustic hot springs, which are reputed to be occasionally visited by "undesirables." The scenery rapidly becomes secluded as you progress upstream past the springs. The trail eventually ascends past the following waterfall.

Jerry Johnson Falls

Drive to the parking area for Warm Springs Creek Trail #49, located one mile east of Jerry Johnson Campground. A footbridge crosses Lochsa River before the trail reaches Warm Springs Creek and follows it upstream 1½ miles to the hot springs. The trail crosses a small tributary creek one mile farther, then gradually ascends above Warm Springs Creek to trailside views of the falls in one mile. The creek below you roars 40 to 70 feet into a basin.

RIGGINS

The town of Riggins is the western gateway to the wild Salmon River. White water boating is extremely exciting along this "River of No Return." Riggins is downstream from most of the float "action," so jetboats carry visitors

Jerry Johnson Falls

up and down the river. For more information on guided excursions, write "White Water," Bureau of Tourism and Industrial Promotion, Room 108, Capitol Building, Boise, Idaho 83720.

Carey Falls

Turn off U.S. 95 onto Salmon River Road. The junction is less than a mile south of Riggins. The road winds with the river for 26 miles to Wind River Pack Bridge. Carey Falls is about half a mile farther upstream, or 1½ miles before the end of the gravel road. This is the final descent along the Salmon River.

GARDEN VALLEY

At the town of Banks, turn off S.R. 55 toward Lowman onto South Fork Road. Drive past Garden Valley Ranger Station in 11 miles. The paved road turns to gravel after a total of 16 miles. Pass many hot springs next to the South Fork Payette River.

Little Falls

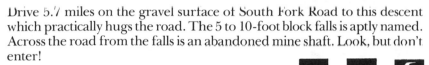

Drive 5.7 miles on the gravel surface of South Fork Road to this descent which practically hugs the road. The 5 to 10-foot block falls is aptly named. Across the road from the falls is an abandoned mine shaft. Look, but don't enter!

Big Falls

This 25 to 40-foot descent is "big" only in contrast with its downstream counterpart. Continue 2.2 miles past Little Falls. Park where the road widens and peer upstream to the canyon floor 100 to 150 feet below.

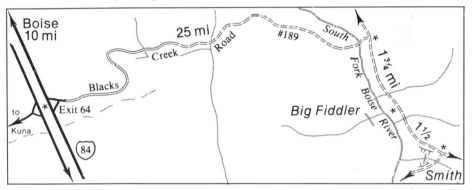

SOUTH FORK BOISE RIVER

Travel through rangeland, over the Danskin Mountains, and into South Fork Canyon. The 300 to 400-foot deep gorge is rarely visited. Turn off Interstate 84 ten miles south of Boise at the Blacks Creek Road/Kuna turnoff (Exit 64). Drive east (away from Kuna) along Blacks Creek Road #189. The road soon turns to gravel, then dirt after ten miles. It is reliable from May to October, but not safe for passenger vehicles during the winter. Cross the Danskin Mountains and reach the South Fork in 21 miles. The road winds into the canyon and crosses the river four miles farther.

Big Fiddler Creek Falls

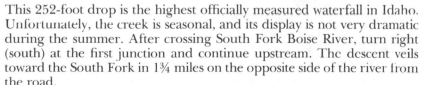

This 252-foot drop is the highest officially measured waterfall in Idaho. Unfortunately, the creek is seasonal, and its display is not very dramatic during the summer. After crossing South Fork Boise River, turn right (south) at the first junction and continue upstream. The descent veils toward the South Fork in 1¾ miles on the opposite side of the river from the road.

Smith Creek Falls

Drive about 1½ miles past the previous entry on Blacks Creek Road # 189. Listen for the falls near where the road leaves the South Fork. The descent is 0.1 mile downstream from the first primitive road crossing the creek. Carefully make your way through sagebrush for clearer views of Smith Creek dropping steeply 150 to 200 feet.

MIDDLE FORK SALMON RIVER

Remoteness is the attraction of a vacation along the Wild and Scenic Middle Fork Salmon River. The river bisects the Idaho Primitive Area on its way to a confluence with the main fork of the Salmon. All but the initial entry can be

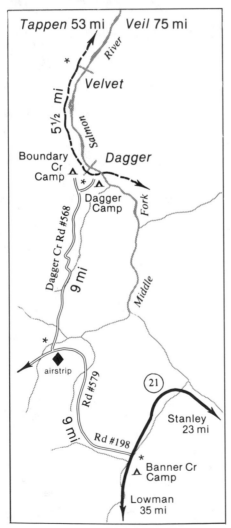

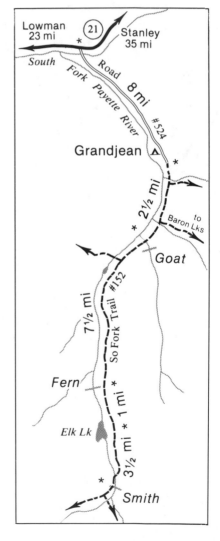

reached only on extensive backcountry excursions. For river guide information, contact "White Water," Bureau of Tourism and Industrial Promotion, Room 108, Capitol Building, Boise 83720. Small craft air service information can be obtained by writing the Idaho Department of Aeronautics, 2103 Airport Way, Boise 83705.

Dagger Falls

This is the only descent along the Middle Fork drainage readily accessible to travelers. Turn off S.R. 21 onto Cape Horn Creek Road #198 just north of Banner Creek Camp. This route ascends over a pass in three miles and becomes Fir Creek Road #579. Six miles farther, across from Bruce Meadows Air Strip, turn right (north) on Dagger Creek Road #568. The campgrounds and the 15-foot descent are at the road's end in 13 miles.

Velvet Falls

This major cascade along the Middle Fork is accessible by water or trail. It is located 5½ miles downstream from Dagger Falls.

Tappen Falls

This series of descents within a half mile stretch of Middle Fork Salmon River is located 8½ miles downstream from Simplot Ranch, or 53 miles past Velvet Falls.

Veil Falls

Look for this unnamed tributary descending on the east canyon wall about two miles past Big Creek, or 22½ miles downstream from Tappen Falls.

SAWTOOTHS WEST

The rugged Sawtooth Mountains are a tribute to the sculpturing of past alpine glaciers. This section and the next three sections describe waterfalls in Sawtooth Wilderness Area. To reach the following three cataracts near the western flank of the mountains, turn off S.R. 21 at the marked access road to Grandjean Camp. Drive eight miles to trailheads at the end of the gravel road.

Goat Creek Falls

Start on South Fork Trail #152, which parallels South Fork Payette River. Hike to the junction of Baron Creek Trail #154 in 1¼ miles and continue to Goat Creek another moderate 1¼ miles farther. Scramble a short distance upstream to a series of cascades totaling 50 feet.

Fern Falls

Continue 7½ miles past the previous entry on South Fork Trail #152 to where South Fork Payette River tumbles twice in an attractive 30-foot display.

Smith Falls

Hike one mile upstream from Fern Falls along South Fork Trail #152 to Elk Lake. The path crosses the river 3½ miles past the lake. Smith Falls, the last named descent on the South Fork Payette, is a short distance upstream.

BARON CREEK

Tohobit Creek Falls

Drive to the Grandjean area as described in the preceding section. Hike 1¼ miles along South Fork Trail #152 to Baron Creek Trail #154. Follow it seven miles to trailside views across the canyon where Tohobit Creek descends into the glacial valley of Baron Creek.

Warbonnet Falls

Continue one mile past the previous trailside vista to another waterfall hurtling from the lip of a hanging valley.

Fern Falls

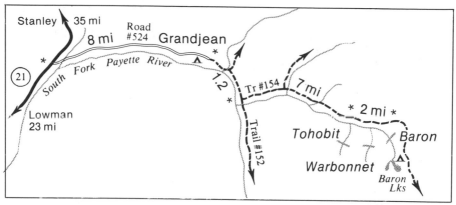

Baron Creek Falls

Baron Creek pours 50 feet down as the stream breaks through a glacial moraine of rock debris. Hike along Baron Creek Trail #154 one mile past views of Warbonnet Falls to this descent. The trail continues up past the twin cataracts toward Baron Lakes.

STANLEY LAKE CREEK

Enter the Sawtooths from the north by driving five miles west of Stanley along S.R. 21. Turn left at Stanley Lake Road and drive 3½ miles to Inlet Camp. The trailhead for Stanley Lake Creek Trail is near Area B of the campground.

Lady Face Falls

Stanley Lake Creek breaks through a moraine and falls 50 to 75 feet into a basin. Follow Stanley Lake Trail for 2½ miles. Look for a sign marking the descent. Retrace your steps if you've passed where the main trail crosses the creek.

Bridal Veil Falls

Hike 1¼ miles past Lady Face Falls to the trail's junction with Hanson Lakes Trail. Nearby are trailside views of the outlet from Hanson Lakes cascading toward Stanley Lake Creek. The route continues up steeply to the lakes in 1¼ miles.

SAWTOOTHS EAST

Goat Falls

Drive 2¼ miles west of Stanley on S.R. 21 to Iron Creek Road. Drive four miles to the end of the gravel road and the beginning of Alpine Lake/Saw-

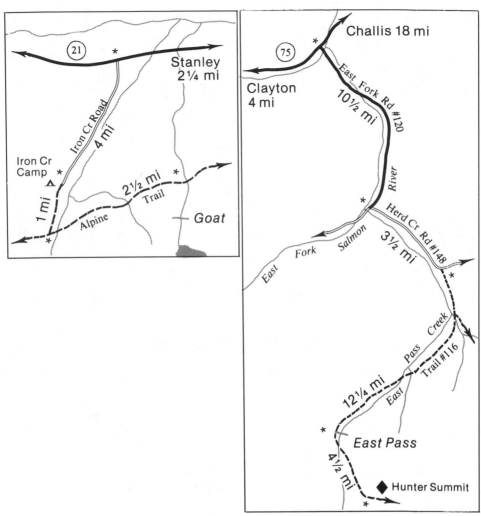

tooth Lake Trail. Turn left (southwest) in one mile at the junction of Alpine Trail. Continue 2½ miles to full views of Goat Creek veiling 250 to 350 feet. Note: This is not the same Goat Creek described in SAW-TOOTHS WEST.

WHITE CLOUD PEAKS

East Pass Creek Falls

Drive four miles east of Clayton on S.R. 75 and turn right (south) on East Fork Salmon River Road #120. After 10½ miles, turn left (southeast) on gravelled Herd Creek Road #148 and drive 3½ miles to the start of Trail #116. Backpack 12¼ miles to the descent. Hunter Summit is 4¼ miles farther.

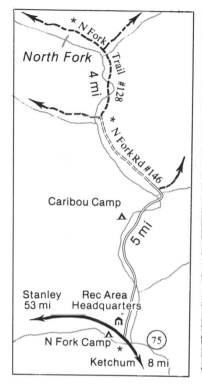

Goat Falls

KETCHUM AREA

North Fork Falls

Drive eight miles north of Ketchum along S.R. 75 to the headquarters of Sawtooth National Recreation Area. Turn right (north) on North Fork Road #146. East Fork crosses over the road after 3½ miles. Check the stream level before attempting to ford the stream with your vehicle. Continue 1½ miles to the end of the road, then hike about four miles along North Fork Trail #128. The trail rises above the canyon floor near where North Fork Big Wood River slides 50 to 75 feet.

TRAIL CREEK PASS

Trail Creek Falls

A few years ago this descent could only be visited by determined bush-wackers. Now a newly constructed trail reportedly passes by the falls. Drive northeast from Ketchum and Sun Valley on Trail Creek Road #51. Reach Trail Creek Summit in 10¼ miles and Park Creek Road #140 three-fourths mile beyond. Turn left (west) on Road #140 and drive

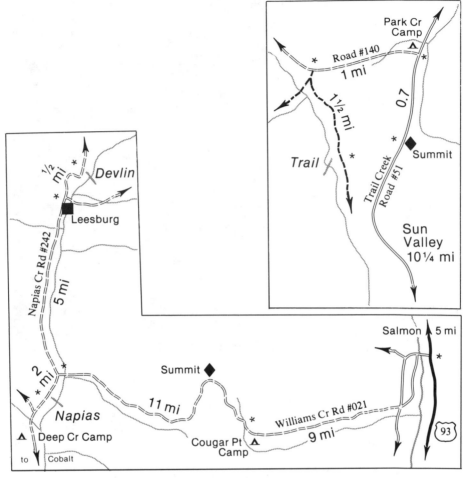

about one mile to a dirt road to the left. The trail should start nearby. It leads 1½ miles downstream to the 60-foot falls.

SALMON NATIONAL FOREST

Two descents tumble along Napias Creek deep in the mining country of Salmon National Forest. Napias is Shoshoni for "money." Prospectors named the stream when placer gold was discovered in it in 1866. Turn off U.S. 93 at Williams Creek Road #021 five miles south of Salmon.

Napias Creek Falls

Drive 20 miles on Williams Creek Road #021 to Napias Creek. Turn left (south) and continue on Road #021 as it follows the creek downstream. A series of cascades totaling 70 feet descends next to the road in about two miles.

Devlin Falls

Leave Williams Creek Road #021 at Napias Creek, turning right (north) on bumpy Napias Creek Road #242. The descent is next to the road 5½ miles farther near the historic townsite of Leesburg. The community was born in the gold rush of 1866 and its population ballooned to 7,000 residents within 12 months. But the rush soon subsided. By 1870 only 180 people lived in Leesburg. Today the site is a mining outpost at best.

SALMON RIVER

The Salmon River has carved a canyon over one mile deep as it flows 165 miles west through the Clearwater Mountains. Adventures await experienced rafters and boaters who accept the challenge of negotiating forty stretches of rapids and cascades along the "River of No Return." Novices should not attempt to run this river. Secure the services of a licensed river guide or outfitter. For further information, write "White Water," Bureau of Tourism and Industrial Promotion, Room 108, Capitol Building, Boise 83720.

There are two named falls in the eastern half of the Salmon River Canyon. One is accessible to motorists, while the other can only be reached by river runners.

Fountain Creek Falls

Turn off U.S. 93 at North Fork and follow Salmon River Road westward. Drive to Shoup in 26 miles and Cache Bar Camp 18 miles farther. Look for the falls half a mile past the campground. Fountain Creek streams from a canyon wall toward the Salmon in a stairstep display. The road ends two miles beyond the falls.

Salmon Falls

Salmon Falls is 1.9 miles downstream from Corey Bar Camp or 21½ miles past where the road ends at Corn Creek campsite. This cascade is one of many which test the boater's mettle.

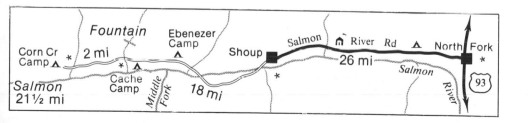

THE SNAKE RIVER PLAIN OF SOUTHERN IDAHO

Southern Idaho presents the traveler with a dilemma. There is no best time of the year to visit its waterfalls. The prime viewing time for individual falls varies more dramatically here than in any other region of the Pacific Northwest.

Streams originating from springs are the least temperamental, since they flow continuously. Jump Creek and the Thousand Springs area offer examples. Some stream flows fluctuate with the demand for hydroelectric power. The falls near Hagerman and Clear lakes are altered by the amount of water being diverted to the nearby power stations. The waterfalls along the Snake River near Twin Falls actually stop flowing most summers! This is because Milner Dam, located farther upstream, impounds water for irrigation of agricultural lands. Some hydro projects along the Snake have destroyed waterfalls. American Falls Dam and Swan Falls Dam have replaced the original descents and the waters of C.J. Strike Reservoir cover *Crane Falls*. The highland waterfalls northeast of Rexburg flow perennially, but are easily accessible during summer only. Cross-country skis or a snowmobile are required for travel from November to May.

The Snake River Plain has 40 recognized falls, of which 33 are described here. The majority of them were created by stream courses eroding across heterogenous bedrock at varying rates. The falls along the Snake formed because bedrock such as rhyolite resists stream erosion more effectively than basalt, its igneous counterpart. Most of the falls in the eastern highland areas were shaped in the same way.

Waterfalls descend from the canyon rims of the Snake River for two reasons. Few streams flow into the river from the solidified lava flows of the Plain, and those that do cannot erode the underlying bedrock material as effectively as the Snake. As a result, waterfalls often drop where streams intersect the canyon rim. Other waterfalls descend from springs along the canyon walls.

JUMP CREEK CANYON

This small canyon is one of Idaho's hidden gems. Drive on U.S. 95 to Poison Creek Road, located 2½ miles south of the junction with S.R. 55. In 3½ miles, where the paved road takes a sharp right, turn left (south) on an unnamed gravel road. Follow it for half a mile, then turn right (west) onto a dirt road. Do not be discouraged if you see a "No Tresspassing" sign. This route is the correct public access to the canyon. In 0.4 mile, the road forks. The low road leads to a private homestead and the high road to the right ends in front of the canyon in one additional mile. The land is administered by the Bureau of Land Management.

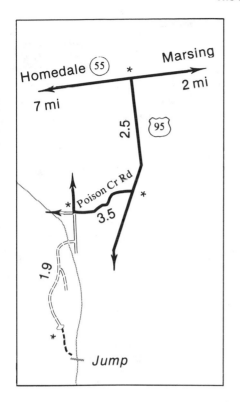

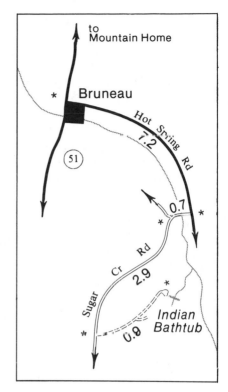

Jump Creek Falls

Follow the pathway along the canyon's floor, hopping from stone to stone across the creek and climbing over, around, and under large boulders which have fallen into the gorge. At the trail's end in 0.2 mile, water splashes 40 to 60 feet into the canyon.

HOT SPRINGS

Indian Bathtub Falls

Although the waterfall is unimpressive, the thermal springs of this area justify a visit. Drive on S.R. 51 to Bruneau, then continue southeast for 7.2 miles along Hot Spring Road. Turn right on the road marked Indian Bathtub, then left in three-fourths mile on the road marked Sugar Creek. In 2.9 miles, turn left (east) on a dirt road which leads 0.6 mile to the parking area near the hot springs.

Warm water trickles down 7 to 12 feet from adjacent bedrock into the basin. It's an excellent place to soak, but wear something on your feet. Careless visitors have left broken glass at the bottom of the pool. Indian Bathtub is on land administered by the Bureau of Land Management.

DEADMAN CANYON

Deadman Falls

This gaping canyon was slowly carved by the erosive powers of seasonal Deadman Creek. Leave Interstate 84 at Glenns Ferry. Drive 1.7 miles west of town along Frontage Road to Sailor Creek Road. Cross the bridge at the Snake River and continue 5.8 miles to the canyon rim.

These falls would be a sight worth seeing if only water flowed over the 125 to 175-foot escarpment. A small Bureau of Land Management dam prevents the creek from plunging into the canyon the majority of the year. Perhaps you could see a good show immediately after an intense rainstorm.

HAGERMAN AREA

The scenic quality of the falls along this section of the Snake River varies sporadically. There are dams and powerplants next to each of the falls, and the amount of water allowed to flow over the natural course is determined by the region's electrical demand. The area is accessible via U.S. 30, also called Thousand Springs Scenic Route.

Lower Salmon Falls

Turn off the Scenic Route at the marked Lower Salmon Power Plant entrance, located 6¾ miles south of Gooding-Hagerman Exit 141 from Interstate 84 or 1½ miles north of downtown Hagerman. Drive about three-fourths mile to the 10 to 15-foot waterfall. It is on the far side of the river below the power plant substation.

Upper Salmon Falls

Water diverges into four main blocks, each descending 15 to 25 feet along the Snake River. Drive 3.2 miles south of Hagerman and turn right (west) at the access sign. If you pass the rest area, you have missed the turnoff. Follow this secondary road 1½ miles to the power plant. There are obscured views of the falls from a gravel road. For closer views, park at the east end of the gravel road and cross an unmarked catwalk to an island halfway across the Snake, then proceed down the cement walkway to the falls. Periodically, the walkway area is flooded by Idaho Power, and the company is not liable if unwary visitors are trapped on the island.

SNAKE PLAINS AQUIFER

The Snake River Plain northeast of Hagerman harbors one of the world's greatest groundwater resources. Mountain ranges southeast of central Idaho receive large amounts of precipitation, particularly during the winter. But the streams flowing south from these mountains fail to reach the Snake River because they sink into lava formations on the plain. Water collects in the

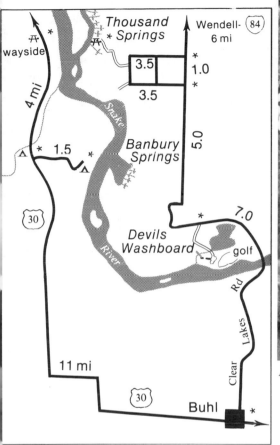

Thousand Springs

wayside

Wendell- 84
6 mi

*

4 mi

3.5 | 1.0

3.5

5.0

Snake

1.5

Banbury Springs

30

River

7.0

Devils Washboard

golf

Rd

Lakes

11 mi

Clear

30

Buhl

Falls from Thousand Springs

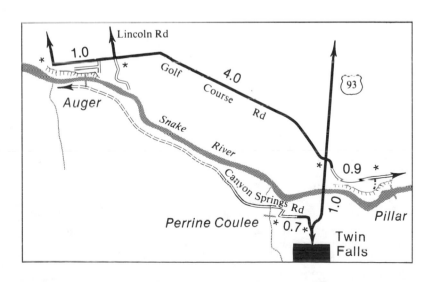

Lincoln Rd

* 1.0 *

Golf

Course

Rd

4.0

93

Auger

Snake

River

0.9

Canyon Springs Rd

1.0

Perrine Coulee

Pillar

0.7

Twin Falls

pore spaces of the subsurface bedrock, and since these rock layers gently dip southwestward, gravity pushes the groundwater toward Hagerman.

The Snake River has eroded its course to intersect with this aquifer. As a result, numerous springs perennially gush from the river's north canyon wall. Most are above the canyon floor, so they are seen as waterfalls descending into the river.

Falls of Thousand Springs

There are eight major falls and many minor falls descending 40 to 100 feet from springs along the north wall on this one-mile stretch of the Snake River Canyon. Astoundingly, the river's volume increases up to tenfold at this point. All the falls can be seen from across the Snake on U.S. 30/Thousand Springs Scenic Route. For a close-up view of the eastern-most descent, turn off from Clear Lakes Road at the sign to Thousand Springs Picnic Area.

Falls of Banbury Springs

Some of these 30 to 80-foot falls can be seen from across the river, but most of them are obscured by the surrounding vegetation. Turn off U.S. 30 and drive to Banbury Hot Springs Resort at the marked access road four miles south of Thousand Springs. The resort is 1½ miles from the main highway.

Devils Washboard Falls

This is a pretty 15 to 30-foot cascade when the adjacent powerhouse isn't diverting most of the water flow from spring-fed Clear Lakes. Drive to the Buhl Country Club seven miles north of Buhl and 12 miles south of Wendell. The waterfall is a short walk west of the country club parking area. At the entrance to the golf course is Clear Lakes Trout Company, reputed to be the world's largest trout farm.

SNAKE RIVER CANYON WEST

The Snake River has carved sharply through basaltic rock layers to create a narrow 400 to 500-foot canyon near Twin Falls. The area has several water-falls.

Auger Falls

Water churns over strange convolutions caused by rocky obstructions along the Snake River. Public views from the north rim are rapidly dwindling as rangeland is converted into housing developments. Turn off Interstate 84 at Exit 168 and drive 3.3 miles south on Lincoln Road, or travel four miles west of U.S. 93 along Golf Course Road to the subdivision area. If you're lucky, you may find an undeveloped lot for sightseeing. Be careful near the rim. For closer views of these 25 to 50-foot cascades, drive about five miles from U.S. 93 along Canyon Springs Road.

Pillar Falls

Towers of 30 to 70-foot rhyolitic rock rise between these 10 to 20-foot cascades along the Snake River. Turn from U.S. 93 at the Golf Course Road sign. Continue along this dusty route for 0.9 mile, then park. Walk through the old dumping grounds for about a quarter mile to the abrupt canyon rim. Pillar Falls is directly below. There is also a distant, yet stunning view of Shoshone Falls. You may wonder about the huge "sandpile" located along the south rim halfway between Pillar Falls and Shoshone Falls. It was the launch site for Evel Knievel's ill-fated attempt to jump the canyon on a "rocket-cycle" during the early 1970s.

Perrine Coulee Falls

Agricultural activities cause this waterfall to flow year-round. In fact, its discharge actually increases during the dry summer! This occurs because the coulee collects water which overflows from the irrigated upland. Turn onto Canyon Springs Road from U.S. 93 and park at the undesignated turnout in less than three-fourths mile. The view is inspiring. A natural pathway goes behind the 197-foot plunge.

SNAKE RIVER CANYON EAST

Twin Falls

Only one of the twin descents remains today. The larger portion has been dammed. Follow Falls Avenue five miles east from the city of Twin Falls, passing the junction to Shoshone Falls. Turn left (north) at the marked road leading one mile to the falls and adjacent picnic area.

A torrent of water hurtles down 125 feet during early spring, but becomes a trickle in summer months. Milner Dam farther upstream draws off a large part of the Snake River for irrigation during the midyear growing season.

Shoshone Falls

This is the most famous waterfall in Idaho. It spans over 1,000 feet across and plunges 212 feet down. The awesome display is best viewed during springtime. Later in the year the river dries up and only large ledges of rhyolite can be seen. The water is diverted upstream for agricultural uses. Backtrack three miles from Twin Falls to the marked turn along Falls Avenue. Shoshone Falls Park is two miles farther.

The following Indian folklore about Shoshone Falls was told in pioneer days to J.S. Harrington by a Shoshoni Indian named Quish-in-demi. It is recorded in *Idaho: A Guide in Words and Pictures,* written in 1937 as part of a Federal Writers' Project:

"In the gloomy gorge above the falls there was, long ago, the trysting place of a deep-chested Shoshoni buck and the slender wild girl whom he loved.

Shoshone Falls

Their last meeting was here on a pile of rocks which overlooked the plunging waters. He went away to scalp with deft incisions and then to lift the shaggy mane of white men with a triumphant shout; and she came daily to stand by the thundering avalanche and remember him. That he would return unharmed she did not, with the ageless resourcefulness of women, ever allow herself to doubt. But time passed, and the moons that came and ripened were many, and she still came nightly to stand on the brink and watch the changeless journeying of the water. And it was here that she stood one black night above the roar of the flood when a warrior stepped out of shadow and whispered to her and then disappeared. As quiet as the flat stone under her feet, she stood for a long while, looking down into the vault where the waters boiled up like seething white hills to fill the sky with dazzling curtains and roll away in convulsed tides. For an hour she gazed down there two hundred feet to a mad pouring of motion and sound into a black graveyard of the dead. And then, slowly, she lifted her arms above her, lifted her head to the fullest curve of her throat, and stood tiptoe for a moment, poised and beautiful, and then dived in a long swift arc against the falling white background.... And the river at this point and since that hour has never been the same."

Bridal Veil Falls

Water tumbles 25 to 40 feet from spring-fed Dierkes Lake in Shoshone Falls Park. The stream nearly sprays onto the road before a culvert directs the water into a pond below.

CITY OF IDAHO FALLS

This low, turbulent descent on the Snake River shares its name with the surrounding community of 40,000. Turn off Interstate 15 at Broadway Street (Exit 118) and drive toward the city center. Immediately before the bridge crossing the Snake, turn left (north) on River Parkway. Stop and enjoy the falls from the adjacent city park.

Idaho Falls of the Snake River

The 15 to 25-foot waterfall is over a quarter mile wide and has the distinction of being man-made! Joe L. Marker, historical editor of the East Idaho tabloid *Post-Register*, explains:

"In the earlier days there were only rapids in the river at Idaho Falls. Then in 1909 during the administration of Mayor Ed Coltman, authorization was given by the city for William Walker Keefer to build a concrete dam in the river to channel some of the stream to the Eagle Rock power plant to generate the turbines for electricity.

"In recent years the dam started to deteriorate, and to assure adequate stream flow for the new bulb turbines in the river here, it was decided to tear out the old dam and rebuild it and the falls, which was undertaken and completed in 1981."

SWAN VALLEY

Fall Creek Falls

Drive 39 miles east of Idaho Falls or 3¼ miles west of Swan Valley along U.S. 26 to the Snake River Road. Follow this gravel route 1.4 miles and park where the road widens. The best views of the falls are a short walk farther along the roadway. Fall Creek plunges 40 to 60 feet into the Snake River. The water plumes upon either side of the central descent to form a natural fountain which must be seen to be believed.

Fall Creek Falls

UPPER PALISADE LAKE

Rainbow Falls

Follow U.S. 26 two miles northeast of the community of Palisades to Palisades Creek Road #254. Turn right and follow the road 1¾ miles to its end at Palisades Campground. Start here on Palisades Creek Trail #84 and hike 7½ miles to Upper Palisade Lake. Bear right at subsequent trail junctions and proceed south into Waterfall Canyon. The tiered waterfall with 80-foot and 30-foot descents is ten miles from the trailhead.

Employees of the Palisades Ranger District, some of who had lived in the area for 40 years, were surprised to learn that the waterfall has a name. I found the title in the 1938 edition of *Idaho Encyclopedia*.

YELLOWSTONE

Although most of the following falls are actually in Wyoming, they have been included here because they can be most easily reached from just across the border in Idaho.

Sheep Falls

The name of this 35-foot waterfall comes from the sheep drives across a bridge which once spanned the Falls River here. Drive six miles from Ashton on S.R. 47 to the marked Cave Falls Road #582. Follow Road #582 for 15¼ miles, then turn right (south) at Wyoming Creek Road #124. This unimproved road ends in four miles at the beginning of Sheep Falls Trail #42. Hike almost two miles to the falls.

Cave Falls

This picturesque block waterfall descends 25 to 35 feet along Falls River within Yellowstone National Park. Travel as to Sheep Falls, but stay on Cave Falls Road #582 to its end at the falls, 20½ miles from S.R. 47. The descent is named after a large recess beneath the stream's left bank.

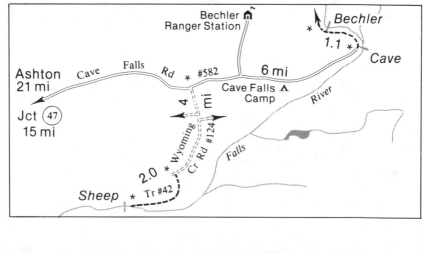

Bechler Falls

Follow the Bechler River Trail for 1.1 miles from Cave Falls to this wide, low descent. The 15 to 25-foot cataract along Bechler River is in Yellowstone National Park.

HENRYS FORK

Henrys Fork is a wild and scenic river in all but official federal designation. It winds through the Ashton Ranger District of Targhee National Forest.

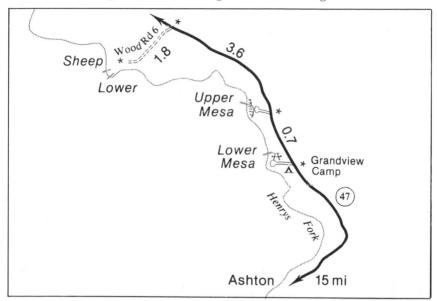

Lower Mesa Falls

Lower Mesa Falls

Peer from an overlook to the rushing water of Henrys Fork over 400 feet below. The river attains a chaotic state while thundering down this 65-foot descent. Drive 15 miles northeast of Ashton on S.R. 47 to the turnout appropriately titled Grandview.

Upper Mesa Falls

For side views of Henrys Fork plummeting 114 feet from a sheer wall of rhyolite rock, turn off S.R. 47 at Upper Mesa Falls Road #295 about three-fourths mile past Grandview. Drive to the road's end in less than one mile. The waterfall, also known as *Big Falls*, is a short walk away. Be careful at the canyon rim!

Lower Falls

Henrys Fork cascades 15 to 25 feet. Drive 4.3 miles past Grandview on S.R. 47 to Wood Road #6. Follow this dirt road as far as your vehicle can follow its 1.8-mile length. No formal trail goes to the river, so pick a safe route down the moderately steep slope.

Sheep Falls

This 15 to 25-foot stairstep along Henrys Fork is less than 100 yards upstream from Lower Falls.

Upper Mesa Falls

INDEX